PRAISE FOR *FRANTZ FANON*

Never before has Frantz Fanon's critique of Negritude been applied with such finesse as by Karthick Ram Manoharan in this bold, fascinating and insightful book, to offer a unique reading of Periyar's anti-caste politics in India, as well as to explicate the logic of the remarkable ongoing Kurdish struggle. In both cases, Fanonian ideas are the wedges used to prise apart the traps of ossified identities, leaving space for articulating the possibility of politically guided 'expansive' identification directed towards a democratic confederalism beyond capitalist nation-states. The book forcefully argues that without a guiding universalism, struggles of minorities become an easy prey for either liberal multiculturalist or right-wing incorporations. Here is a unique book in comparative political philosophy: lucidly and engagingly written, theoretically robust and truly global in its scope.

Meena Dhanda, Professor of Philosophy and Cultural Politics, University of Wolverhampton, UK

This original study places and re-establishes Fanon's critical universalism and humanism in light of ongoing debates over identity politics, nationalism, and multiculturalism. It creatively explores Fanon's critique of forms of national or racial identity that fall short of reaching for 'a world of reciprocal recognitions' – that is, a new humanism that engenders the social deconstruction of race, ethnic, and national particularism. Especially important is the re-reading of Fanon in light of caste as a social phenomenon.

Peter Hudis, Professor of Humanities and Philosophy, Oakton Community College, Illinois, US

LITERARY/CULTURAL THEORY

FRANTZ FANON

Literary/Cultural Theory provides concise and lucid introductions to a range of key concepts and theorists in contemporary literary and cultural theory. Original and contemporary in presentation, and eschewing jargon, each book in the series presents to students of humanities and social sciences exhaustive overviews of theories and theorists, while also introducing them to the mechanics of reading literary/cultural texts using critical tools. Each book also carries glossaries of key terms and ideas, and pointers for further reading and research. Written by scholar-teachers who have taught critical theory for years, and vetted by some of the foremost experts in the field, the series Literary/Cultural Theory is indispensable to students and teachers.

Also in the series

Psychoanalytic Theory and Criticism
Feminisms
Jacques Lacan
Dalit Literature and Criticism
Ecocriticism
Postcolonialism Now
Modernisms
Marxist Literary and Cultural Theory
Postmodernisms
Mikhail Bakhtin
Popular Culture
Diaspora Theory and Transnationalism
Queer Studies

LITERARY/CULTURAL THEORY

FRANTZ FANON

IDENTITY AND RESISTANCE

KARTHICK RAM MANOHARAN
Centre for Studies in Social Sciences, Calcutta (CSSSC)

Edited by
ALLEN HIBBARD
Middle Tennessee State University, Tennessee, US

Orient BlackSwan

FRANTZ FANON

ORIENT BLACKSWAN PRIVATE LIMITED

Registered Office
3-6-752 Himayatnagar, Hyderabad 500 029, Telangana, India
Email: centraloffice@orientblackswan.com

Other Offices
Bengaluru, Bhopal, Chennai, Guwahati, Hyderabad, Jaipur, Kolkata, Lucknow, Mumbai, New Delhi, Noida, Patna, Visakhapatnam

First published 2019

ISBN 978 93 5287 687 7

030139

Typeset in Aldine 401 BT 10.5/13 *by*
Akhil Offset Printers
Hyderabad 500 020

Printed at
Graphica Printers & Binders, Hyderabad 500 013

Published by
Orient Blackswan Private Limited
3-6-752, Himayatnagar,
Hyderabad 500 029, Telangana, India
Email: info@orientblackswan.com

Contents

Editor's Preface

Recent developments in theory have made us keenly aware of how our subject positions affect our ideologies and worldviews. Our class, our gender, our age, our geographical location, our place in history, our ethnic or national identifications, our race, our bodies – all go into shaping who we are, what we think, and how others perceive us. These considerations are especially helpful and relevant as we consider the work of Frantz Fanon. His origins and subsequent journeys unquestionably affected the development of his thought which often centred on ways of breaking through the limitations of particular personal and historical circumstances.

Fanon was born in the French colony of Martinique in 1925. During the Second World War he joined the Free French Forces and made his way to France via Algeria. His first major work, *Black Skin, White Masks,* written in France and published in 1952, was informed by his encounters with strident forms of racism both during and after the war. While in France, Fanon trained as a psychiatrist and read the works of Jean-Paul Sartre, who became a central influence on his thinking. In 1953, Fanon was appointed to a position at the Blida-Joinville Psychiatric Hospital in Algeria, just before the country was thrown into a violent struggle for independence. His work exposed him directly to the effects of torture at the hands of the French. He joined the FLN (Front de Libération Nationale) and severed ties with the occupying power. In the writing of his second important work, *The Wretched of the Earth* (1961), he drew upon his profound understanding of the crippling effects of colonialism, gained from his experiences in Algeria. He died in 1961 in Maryland, USA, where he was undergoing treatment for leukemia. Whenever I think of Fanon's life and work, I am amazed at how much he packed into such a brief span of time, and how substantial his legacy has been.

As Karthick Ram Manoharan aptly notes, Fanon was 'a perennial outsider throughout his political life'. In Martinique, he remained a colonial subject. In France his skin colour marked him as Other. And as much as he immersed himself in the Algerian independence movement, he was neither Algerian nor Muslim. His position as an outsider, as well as the trajectory of his movement, no doubt can be credited for his insights. His experiences made him aware of how one's identity – particularly identity imposed by those in a dominant position – could scar and debilitate a person. From these experiences came a yearning to transcend oppressive social, political and cultural forces that drive wedges between people.

The story of Fanon's reception and influence over the more than half century following his death is fascinating. That his views on race and colonisation continue to absorb our attention is not surprising since we continue to strive for racial justice and deal with the aftermath of colonialism in West Asia, Africa, Asia and elsewhere. Fanon's assertion that '[i]f we really want to safeguard our countries from regression, paralysis, or collapse, we must rapidly switch from a national consciousness to a social and political consciousness' (142) resonates especially forcefully in times when ecological disaster threatens, posing a collective challenge. His sense of commitment and his plain and direct prose no doubt also account for his enduring legacy. His writing is clear, compelling and urgent, even as he grapples with complex issues.

In this volume Manoharan provides us with a sure and reliable introduction to Fanon's work, laying out Fanon's story and the story of his work's reception, accounting for his importance in the history of theory and criticism, arguing for the relevance of his ideas in our contemporary scene, and submitting applications of Fanonian thinking to particularly thorny cases of resistance to oppression. He describes his own first encounter with *The Wretched of the Earth*, struck by its revolutionary message and advocacy of violence, and traces the evolution of his thought. 'The quest, then, is for coherence in Fanon's corpus', he writes in the opening chapter. Throughout his rich and thoughtful discussions, Manoharan draws on both Fanon's better-known works and lesser-known writings such as *Toward the African Revolution* and *Alienation and Freedom*. There may be those who will resist Manoharan's interpretations, yet if they read this volume carefully, they will see how he arrived at his views, through careful reading and rereading of Fanon's oeuvre. Manoharan's logic and prose (like Fanon's) are lucid and transparent. His fervent quest for authenticity may too owe something to Fanon.

As Manoharan notes, there is a Rashomon-like quality to Fanon's work and ideas. Like in a Rorschach blot, readers are apt to interpret his writing to fit their own positions and agendas. In an age of identity politics, Fanon has been seized upon and used by various critics to support their positions. Manoharan takes us through some of these interpretations, seeking to dust off and restore what he takes to be the true Fanon. His is not a Fanon that simply champions one identity (for example, Black, Algerian) over another. Rather, his is a Fanon who ultimately – as he reveals dynamics of oppression – promotes a kind of 'insurgent universalism', involving a dialectic between the particular and the universal that at once acknowledges identities created from and in particular circumstances, yet moves toward the possibility of 'expansive identity', a notion of a more permeable identity that allows subjects flexibility in shaping and transcending themselves in ways that potentially include the Other rather than see the Other as enemy.

Fanon's position on identity politics, as presented by Manoharan, was articulated clearly a couple of decades ago by Ihab Hassan: 'Excessive particularism not only stymies value judgments but also, more drastic to human communities, inhibits the faculty of human empathy, without which no reciprocity is possible' (66). Political systems built on notions of identity politics and multiculturalism inevitably become fractured, and meaningful, radical structural change is elided. Even as Fanon saw no viable alternative to violent strategies to extricate colonialism (because it was so deeply engrained), that approach was not based on an indiscriminate attack on individuals wholly on the basis of their identity (for example, white, Tibetan, Bahá'í). Recent tragic events in Sri Lanka, the United States, New Zealand, and elsewhere – in which members of particular religious groups were targeted for attack – should make the need for a Fanonian-based approach to political conflict even more apparent and urgent.

If there is any one consistent, fundamental principle in Fanon's thinking, it is his opposition to oppression, whatever form it may take. The term 'oppositional humanism' may indeed appropriately characterise his thinking. Along the lines of Sartre, Fanon advocates 'Freedom for All', based on mutual recognition from a position of mutual respect, if not equality. This is a necessary move in deconstructing the master/slave dialectic. In chapter 5, Manoharan writes, 'A truly transformative praxis must unsettle the identity of both the Self and the Other so as to create a new paradigm of discourse where there can be a reconciliation of interests of the actors involved'.

After laying out general contours of Fanon's work and situating it within current debates and controversies, in chapter 3, Manoharan assesses Fanon's views on the notion of negritude, particularly as presented and promoted by West Indies writer Aimé Césaire and Senegalese intellectual and political leader Léopold Sédar Senghor. While he was certainly aware of and influenced by these writers, Manoharan argues that Fanon develops a critique of negritude as a way of dealing with issues of racial difference and conflict, pointing to its essentialist basis, its mythologising of the past, and its lack of revolutionary power.

Especially original and innovative are the final two chapters and the conclusion. Chapter 4, 'Anti-Casteist Castism? A Fanonist Study of Anti-Caste Politics', discusses the work of the radical social reformer from Tamil Nadu in south India, 'Periyar' E. V. Ramasamy, and considers what light Fanon might shed on resistance to the caste system. A system of oppression deeply entrenched within Indian culture, pre-dating colonialism, as Manoharan notes, the caste system is especially difficult to dislodge, posing greater obstacles than elites as Fanon imagines them in a postcolonial Algeria. Manoharan's critique, like Periyar's, begins with a recognition of the brahmin's intransigence. Unlike colonialism, casteism is not a form of oppression imposed from outside; indeed, perhaps a bit paradoxically, colonialism may have somewhat unsettled the system. And unlike in the struggle against colonialism, there exists no indigenous humanistic tradition on which to build a critique of casteism. (How does one develop a dynamic of mutual recognition when one refuses to look at the other or consider him human?) Space thus is needed to speculate a 'universal' beyond brahmin identity, an identity that is at once collective and inclusive. 'Basing a politics on a history of oppression by the Other *alone* cannot produce a transformative praxis to create a more accommodating future and a post-casteist society', Manoharan writes towards the end of the chapter.

Chapter 5 contains a discussion of Fanon's thinking in relation to the on-going struggle for Kurdish autonomy. Drawing on the writings of the PKK (Kurdish Workers' Party) leader Abdullah Öcalan, Manoharan describes a liberation movement that is not bound by identity, but rather works against all forms of oppression, including class structure, religious authoritarianism, sectarian chauvinism, and gender inequality. Thus, the movement seems to be quite compatible with Fanon's views.

Finally, in the conclusion, Manoharan offers a critique of interracial porn and a reading of the recent film *Black Panther* through a Fanonian perspective that challenges pro-Negritude values and – again – stresses the need for a universalism that transcends identity politics.

Good criticism lures us back to particular texts with which we may or may not be familiar. May Karthick Ram Manoharan's energetic, intelligent discussion of Fanon's work incite a fresh wave of Fanon readers. This volume is a superb example of one avid reader's journey with Fanon. Your own journeys through and alongside Fanon, marked by your own particular circumstances, will surely spark self-discovery, spur on your thinking, and stimulate your intellectual growth. This is what happens when we wrestle with angels.

Allen Hibbard

REFERENCES

Fanon, Frantz. *The Wretched of the Earth*. Trans. Richard Philcox. New York: Grove Press, 2004. Print.

Hassan, Ihab. 'Globalism and Its Discontents: Notes of a Wandering Scholar'. *Profession* (1999): 59–67. Print.

Acknowledgements

A good portion of this book is based on my thesis, *To Explain the Other to Myself: Fanon, Ramasamy, and Identity Politics*, submitted for a PhD at the University of Essex in 2015. The idea for this research emerged from a term paper that I presented on Fanon in Neeladri Bhattacharya's class in 2010, when I was pursuing my MA in History at the Jawaharlal Nehru University (JNU), New Delhi. When I discussed the possibility of a comparative study of Fanon and Periyar with M. S. S. Pandian, he encouraged it with much enthusiasm and guided me in shaping a solid research proposal.

I applied to the University of Essex and I joined the Department of Government in 2011 as a PhD student, with a generous grant from the University of Essex Scholarship. David Howarth, my supervisor, and Aletta Norval, who was on my advisory board, provided me excellent guidance that helped me successfully complete and defend my thesis. Ravi Vaithees, the external examiner for my viva, and Laura Montanaro, the internal examiner, provided several important inputs which improved my work. My friends on campus, and the academic and non-academic staff, made my stay at Essex memorable.

The Centre for Studies in Social Sciences (CSSSC) provided me the best possible atmosphere to work on this book. I am grateful to my colleagues for their warm support. Debarshi Sen, the Registrar, Rosinka Chaudhuri, the Director, and Tapati Guha-Thakurta, the former Director, were ever ready to help and promote a young academic. A special thanks to Manas Ray for his detailed feedback on a paper on Fanon that I had presented at the 2016 Cultural Studies Workshop, and to Partha Chatterjee for clarifying several confusions around Hegel over many discussions. I have enjoyed several productive conversations with Maidul, Rajarshi and Satish on questions of class, caste, religion and identity. I also learnt much from interacting with my colleagues Anirban, Asha, Debdatta,

Kiran, Lakshmi, Manabi, Prachi, Priya and Trina. Some portions of this book were presented as lectures to my students and I am thankful for their questions and comments. I must also thank my friends at Azim Premji University, where I worked for a short but unforgettable period, for many insightful conversations.

I am grateful to Padmaja Anant and S. Sreenath from Orient BlackSwan for their enthusiastic response to my book proposal and for assisting me throughout the process. Allen Hibbard was a remarkable series editor who took an intense personal interest in this book, providing me excellent feedback at every step. His support and encouragement helped shape the book as it is today.

Interactions with several Tamil and Kurdish diaspora intellectuals and activists in the West helped me understand identity and resistance better and read Fanon in a manner that was relevant today. Being acquainted with Jeyachandran, Krisna, Lathan and Malathy gave me valuable insights into the dynamics of movements for self-determination. Fr. Elil gifted me *Being and Nothingness* and other books relevant to my research, along with his blessings. International Initiative promptly sent me works on the Kurdish movement on request. Murali and I have had several discussions on subjects related to those covered in this book over dinner at his place in London, where his family hosted me with much affection. Anandhi, Kalaiyarasan and Vijayabaskar have been great friends, mentors and well-wishers. I continue to learn much from them.

My family was a formidable pillar of strength to me. The care of Kammu, Thatha and Granny always gave me warmth and comfort. Vilasini, besides being a loving partner, constantly challenged me intellectually and made me reconsider quite some of my views over several memorable arguments. Sathyadev was an endless source of joy.

I am indebted for life to P. E. Manoharan and Durga Lakshmi Manoharan, my father and mother, who provided for me and for my education way beyond the means of a Tamil middle-class family. Living up to your faith in me and making you proud is both my greatest motivation and reward. My first book is a result of your sacrifices and is dedicated to your love.

Karthick Ram Manoharan

Chapter One

Reading Fanon Today

Why invoke Frantz Fanon today, quite out of historical context?

Homi K. Bhabha

I first read Frantz Fanon in 2008. It was a turbulent time for me as a Tamil student–activist. In Sri Lanka, a country not far from my home in south India, the Tamil resistance was making a desperate last stand against the no-holds-barred onslaught by the government. Thousands of Tamils in the Indian state of Tamil Nadu were on the streets, protesting against Sri Lanka's brutal military campaign. In that period, *The Wretched of the Earth* (*WOTE*) was intellectual dynamite to me. 'Violence can thus be understood to be the perfect mediation. The colonized man liberates himself in and through violence,' Fanon said in incendiary prose (44). Reading this work in those times, his relatively simple (so it then appeared) first chapter on violence appealed to me more than the other chapters, which required more nuance than what I had at that time. My Fanon was a Manichean, who stood against the violence of the oppressor, and legitimised the violence of the oppressed. Like several of his admirers across the Third World who had *only* read *WOTE*, I too read him as a prophet of anti-colonial violence. His exhortations for a relentless struggle seemed to be the only sensible option in a hopelessly unjust world.

Travelling with Fanon as an academic, I discovered an extremely complex thinker with penetrating insights on a variety of topics, but I chose a singular theme for my research, which was also a key concern for Fanon – identity. Reading Fanon in reverse, from *WOTE* to his first book *Black Skin, White Masks* (*BSWM*), I could clearly demarcate a pre-Algeria Fanon of *BSWM* from the later Fanon of *WOTE* who was witness to the brutalities of French colonialism in Algeria. The early Fanon, a Black Martinician in white France, was exposed to the racist prejudices and fantasies of the white French. *BSWM* emerges as a brilliant analysis of white racism as well as a merciless satirisation of the search for a Black authenticity, namely, Negritude. *BSWM* is Fanon at his Hegelian-Sartrean finest (though these influences can be traced in his later works too). *WOTE* was written in much hurry while Fanon lay dying of leukemia at the age of thirty-seven. *BSWM* was written in better times, by a younger Fanon, who had time and the resources of Lyon on his side. It is witty, poetic, epigrammatic and incisive. *WOTE,* on the other hand, is angry, powerful and blunt. To draw a crude parallel, compare a scalpel with a sledgehammer.

Homi K. Bhabha, who played no small role in popularising Fanon in the Anglo-Saxon academia, prefers the younger Fanon of *BSWM* to the Fanon of *WOTE*. In his foreword to the 1986 English edition of *BSWM*, Bhabha writes, 'Fanon is not principally posing the question of political oppression as the violation of a human essence, although he lapses into such a lament in his more existential moment' ('Remembering Fanon' xxv). Fanonist activist–scholar Nigel Gibson, who takes an opposing position, chooses the Fanon of *WOTE*, empathising with the thinker's call for a radical decolonisation, if necessary through violence, terming this a 'new humanism' (*Fanon* 174). David Macey captures this conflict in his authoritative biography of Fanon: 'The Third Worldist Fanon was an apocalyptic creature; the post-colonial Fanon worries about identity politics, and often about his own sexual identity, but he is no longer angry. And yet, if there is truly a Fanonian emotion, it is anger' (28).

Macey would also say that '[t]he combination of anger and generosity of spirit is his true legacy' (505). In as much as Fanon could be characterised by his anger towards the coloniser, and his impatience towards the fence-sitting liberal intellectuals of Europe, he was also generous towards the European Other, and believed in the possibility of love. This is not love as a mere humanitarian gesture, but a radical love that believed in the transformation of the Self and the Other. In Hegelese, a love that 'deprives the other of its *foreign* or *alien* character' (Williams 79; italics in original). Fanon thus asks in the conclusion of *BSWM:* 'Was my freedom not given to me then in order to build the world of the You?' (181).

The wider appeal of *WOTE* cannot be underestimated. Movements across the world were inspired by *WOTE*. Several intellectuals and activists swearing allegiance to the Civil Rights Movement in the US, Black Power, Black Lives Matter, indigenous people's movements in Latin America, anti-apartheid movement in South Africa and later the Abahlali baseMjondolo, the uprising in Palestine and others have claimed this work to be an inspiration. This indeed was worrying for the liberal intelligentsia. In her remarkable work *On Violence,* Hannah Arendt was deeply concerned about the manner in which the subject is addressed by Fanon, though she found the Sartrean perspective even more disturbing. Arendt was perturbed by *WOTE*'s 'great influence on the present student generation'; she nevertheless clarified that 'Fanon himself, however, is much more doubtful about violence than his admirers' (14). Such was its lucidity and passion that even an apostle of non-violence like Martin Luther King Jr. called it a 'well-written book, incidentally, with many penetrating insights' (329), even as he chided the Black Power movement for taking this work out of context.

CONTEXT

Frantz Fanon was born on 20 July 1925 to Caisimir and Eléanore Fanon. He was the fifth of eight children in an upper-middle-class family in the French colony of Martinique. His father was largely absent and his mother favoured his sisters over him. As a child, Fanon was mostly close to his elder brother Joby. Fanon did not encounter the severity of racism till his teenage years. In 1939, when Pétainist forces under Admiral Georges Robert took over Martinique, the Fanons witnessed the cruelties of military occupation first-hand. But it was Frantz who would be compelled into action by this. In full earnest, he joined the anti-Fascist forces under de Gaulle, despite Black Martinician thinkers urging the natives to not join the 'white man's war'. Fanon's response was sharp – 'whenever human dignity and freedom are at stake, it involves us, whether we be black, white or yellow' (Cherki 10). This spirit of universalism and solidarity would inform all of Fanon's works.

But a racist society did not reciprocate. Suffering discrimination in the French Army by the white soldiers despite his commitment to France in the anti-Fascist war, Fanon would return home embittered, but still not cynical. Before leaving for Paris, he told his elder brother, 'One must constantly, Joby, put one's life in accord with one's ideas. No excuse is allowable, or one becomes nothing but a worthless bastard' (qtd. in Ehlen 51). When he enrolled to study psychiatry in Lyon, he also immersed himself in works of literature and (largely European) philosophy. He read Hegel, Nietzsche, Marx, Freud, Lacan, Merleau-Ponty and Kojève. But his greatest intellectual influence was Jean-Paul Sartre, whom he would later call a 'living god'. Yet, to the white French around him, Fanon was an object of curiosity, perverse fascination and irrational fear. The Black man who speaks perfect French! The gaze of the white Other confined him to his Black skin. The struggle against this gaze and its determination would form a core subject of *BSWM*, published in 1952, six years after Fanon arrived in Lyon. Fanon was twenty-eight.

BSWM is important for understanding the later Frantz Fanon. Contrary to what Bhabha opined, political oppression *is* posed by Fanon as a principal factor of the denial of human worth. Fanon talks about colonial racism and its pernicious effects on the psyche of the colonised. While *BSWM* is the work that engages most with psychoanalytic thought, he argues that the presence of neuroses and inferiority complex in a patient in the colony is the result of a racist society 'that derives its stability from the perpetuation of this complex, in a society that proclaims the superiority of one race', and that the duty of the psychoanalyst is also to enable the patient to dismantle such a society' (74). It is precisely such a political concern that would later guide his work as a doctor in Algeria. In *BSWM*, Fanon navigates through philosophy, psychoanalysis and literature to arrive at a diagnosis of racism. But the good Doctor Fanon does not believe that Negritude, the poetics and politics of

Black assertion and separation, is a solution. Dissecting the search for an authentic Blackness and a Black civilisation as an antidote to whiteness, Fanon draws his inspiration from the future. Like the existentialists, Sartre in particular, he states his commitment to the freedom of the individual: 'I am not a prisoner of history. I should not seek there for the meaning of my destiny' (179). Freedom would not be found in a narcissistic enclosed identity, but only in an expansive struggle. He would find that not in Paris, not among the Negritude poets, but elsewhere in the African continent in a predominantly Arab country.

In 1953, Fanon set off to Algeria. He would serve at the Blida-Joinville hospital for three years. Appalled at the conditions there and protesting against the condescending manner in which French doctors treated Arab patients, he tried to introduce a method of sociotherapy which aimed to 'construct a new social arena in which the broken thread of personal suffering can be salvaged and expressed' (Cherki 65). This stemmed from a conviction, expressed earlier in *BSWM*, that the neurosis of patients in the colony was not individual but social in nature. In this period, Fanon also became completely convinced that any humane reform of French colonialism was impossible. It was a violent system and it could be ejected only by violence.

In 1954, the National Liberation Front (Front de Libération Nationale, FLN), an Algerian nationalist party, was formed. The FLN was not a romantic revolutionary movement, an image one is likely to form if one reads Fanon uncritically, but was a pragmatic nationalist party that waged a ruthless insurgency. They planned tactical operations to provoke brutal reprisals from the French colonialists. In the Battle of Philippeville in August 1955, the FLN swooped down into the small town and killed several dozens of French settlers, soldiers and civilians alike. Women and children were raped before being executed. The French retaliated by summarily executing hundreds of Algerians suspected of aiding the FLN. The result of this event was a radicalisation of common Algerians, swelling the ranks of the FLN. They needed an intellectual to represent them. They heard of a Black French-speaking psychiatrist in Blida, and contacted him.

For well over a year Fanon treated Algerian militants in his clinic. This included training them to withstand torture which was a fundamental part of French counterinsurgency operations. Fanon's open affiliation with the FLN and the increase in armed conflict made Algeria unsafe for him – indeed, even white French activists who were sympathetic to the FLN were tortured and killed by the colonial military. In 1956, Fanon submitted his resignation letter to the resident French minister, where he termed the French occupation of Algeria 'a systematized de-humanization' (*Toward the African Revolution* 53). He left for Tunisia the same year, transiting through Paris. He was appointed as the spokesperson for the FLN in 1957.

While *WOTE* was a work that looked to the future, it was *A Dying Colonialism* (*ADC*) that captured the present of the Algerian struggle as Fanon saw it. And like *WOTE*, this too has a controversial chapter – 'Algeria Unveiled' – which both critics and supporters of Fanon have understood as a de facto endorsement of the veil worn by Algerian Muslim women as a symbol of resistance against colonialism. In the wake of the so-called 'burqa bans' in some European countries today, one can understand why such a reading still has currency. However, Fanon also envisaged a situation where the veil would be abandoned 'in the course of revolutionary action' (*ADC* 63). A more important chapter in my opinion is the one on 'Algeria's European Minority' where Fanon, the analyst of revolutionary anti-colonial violence, calls for an integration of Europeans in Algeria into the liberation struggle on an ethic of solidarity, eschewing any form of resentful ethnic hatred. While the reality was rather different – the FLN massacred hundreds of French civilians in response to the colonial violence that killed thousands of Arabs – Fanon believed in the possibility of a political commitment to a common cause trumping ethnic affiliations. This too was informed by a belief in a new humanism. One could say that Fanon had an almost childlike faith in the transformative potential of the anti-colonial struggle: colonialism's forces are drowned by the 'overwhelming moral superiority of the Algerian revolution' (*Alienation and Freedom* 545) and the French soldiers themselves are compelled to join the FLN's ranks. 'By opening up its arms to them, the Algerian Revolution not only delivers them from their oppressor but cures them of this atrocious evil; the revolution liberates their chained up consciences and awakens their intelligence to the grand human ideals it defends' (545).

Toward the African Revolution (*TAR*) is a partial collection of articles written by Fanon from the time he arrived in Algeria to his last days on the African continent. Most of these articles were published anonymously in the FLN mouthpiece *El moudjahid.* If *BSWM* saw Fanon satirising Negritude, *TAR* saw his decisive break with it. Controversially, again, he wrote, that '[t]he truth is that there is nothing, *a priori,* to warrant the assumption that such a thing as a Negro people exists' (*TAR* 18), and dubbed the Negritude movement 'the great black mirage' (27). Fanon represented the FLN at the First Conference of the Union of African Nations held at Accra, Ghana, in December 1958. Where others saw an intelligent Black-African, Fanon saw in himself an Algerian militant fighting for the cause of an African unity – a unity not built on imagined civilisational pasts or rigid notions of ethnicity, but a political unity based on an opposition to colonialism and a commitment to build a progressive, egalitarian society. He had written more in this period; the complete hitherto unpublished works of Fanon would be compiled and released in English only in 2018. Edited by Jean Khalfa and Robert J. C. Young, this collection, aptly titled *Alienation and Freedom* (*AF*), as a nod to Fanon's commitment to existentialist themes, contains his literary writings from his earlier days, his clinical writings and the political articles of the later Fanon. These new writings do not offer a significantly new insight that would radically alter the way Fanon can be read but they reaffirm his commitment to universal values and his profound distaste for a narrow form of identitarianism. His letter to Ali Shariati Mazinani, one of the key thinkers of the Iranian Islamic revolution, is evidence of his suspicion of political Islam (*AF* 667–70). To Fanon, 'if it is good to have a tradition, it is also agreeable to be able to go beyond that tradition and invent a new mode of being' (*AF* 283).

Fanon delivered a lecture in Rome at the Congress of Black Writers and Artists in June 1959 on the role of national culture in anti-colonialism that would form one of the chapters of *WOTE.*

The next month, there would be an assassination attempt on Fanon in the same city. Little did the assassins know that in about a year, a more efficient killer would strike this formidable enemy of French colonialism. In December 1960, a fatigued Fanon underwent a series of blood tests. The diagnosis was leukemia. Tunis, where Fanon was staying at the end of his life, did not have adequate facilities to treat him. He was sent to Moscow, where the Soviets suggested that he travel to the US for treatment. Yet, there was a pilgrimage he had to take before he travelled across the seas to the 'country of lynchers'.

Returning from Moscow, Fanon began work on *WOTE*. In this period he met the French filmmaker Claude Lanzmann, a close friend of Sartre and Beauvoir. When the latter inquired about his health, Fanon stated his interest to talk about something else – about Sartre and his works (Cherki 160). Lanzmann would be instrumental in arranging the meeting between Fanon, Sartre and Beauvoir in April 1961. Fanon would finally meet his living god in person in Rome.

SARTRE

Fanon talked to Sartre for hours at a stretch, from lunch to the early hours of the next day. Though weakened by disease, he refused to take a break in conversation. When Beauvoir, who noticed that Sartre was quite exhausted, suggested that they stop for the day, Fanon remarked that he did not like those who hoarded their resources. He later told Lanzmann that he would even give 20,000 francs a day 'to be able to talk to Sartre from morning to night for two weeks' (Beauvoir 606). Fanon's fascination for Sartre was unsurprising. One of the greatest European philosophers of the twentieth century, a prolific writer who made offending the powerful and voicing for the powerless the commitment of a lifetime, Sartre was one of the rare French intellectuals of his period who explicitly, vociferously, and even violently, defended the cause of anti-colonialism. Right-wingers engineered rallies calling for him to be hanged. Sartre also escaped a major assassination attempt by a French paramilitary group when his apartment was bombed in 1961.

Fanon, while not an uncritical admirer, did view Sartre with considerable adulation. In December 1959, when Fanon's assistant Marie-Jeanne Manuellan had planned a Christmas party, Fanon asked her why she had not invited him. She said that there would be French people there and Fanon might not like it. Fanon replied, 'Well, if they are like Sartre, I'm not against it' (Aubenas, Web, n. p.). In a letter to François Maspero dated 20 July 1960, he praised *Critique of Dialectical Reason* and expressed his gratitude to Sartre for having provided him 'such great intellectual satisfaction and a better understanding of things' (*AF* 685). One can say that Fanon's attitude towards Sartre corresponded to his attitude towards Europe as such. Fanon did not reject the European intellectual tradition or the emancipatory values in it. He was opposed to the hypocrisy of European colonialism which used a false mask of universalism to dehumanise the people of the colony. He was not opposed to universalism per se – Fanon was a stringent critic of nativist particularism. He located himself, intellectually, in the existentialist-humanist tradition of Sartre. It is a pity that some Fanon scholars want to downplay or even deny Sartre's influence on his thought. This is epistemic identitarianism at its worst.

After their meeting, Sartre readily agreed to write the foreword for *WOTE*. The product would be one of the most memorable essays to be written by the existentialist thinker. As Arendt would later complain, it was a lot more violent than the actual text (12). While violence forms only one chapter of *WOTE*, violence is the key theme of Sartre's foreword. Sartre writes, 'killing a European is killing two birds with one stone, eliminating in one go oppressor and oppressed: leaving one man dead and the other man free' (lv). Shocking indeed. But that was Sartre's purpose – to shock the average French reader from their stupor. He states his intention clearly in the foreword, when he addresses his fellow citizens: 'you who know all the crimes committed in our name, it is really not right not to breathe a word about them to anybody, not even to your own soul, for fear of having to pass judgment on yourselves' (lxii). He wanted to show the French that the systemic crimes of colonialism, in which they were complicit, were fundamentally dehumanising – the terror that emerged in retaliation was the only way the colonised could regain their humanity. Sartre amplified Fanon's voice in a society where he had considerable influence. Sartre's foreword was an insider of France shouting out to his fellows what Fanon had analysed from the outside.

LEGACY

Fanon wanted to die fighting for the independence of Algeria – instead, he died writing about it. *WOTE* was written (actually, dictated by Fanon) in ten weeks. A voluble critic of Western imperialism, Fanon breathed his last under the eyes of the CIA in an American hospital in Maryland. His wife Josie and son Olivier were present beside him. His body was taken to Algeria on a special flight. When *WOTE* was published by Maspero and released in Paris, the French police raided bookstores and seized copies. That would be the last time Fanon's name created a stir in France. In Paris and in Algiers today, he is only occasionally remembered. At Fanon's funeral, Algerian leader Krim Belkacem vowed that Algeria would not forget him. Independent Algeria, however, committed precisely the mistakes that Fanon had warned about in *WOTE*.

Algeria would win formal freedom the next year. The remaining French civilians in Algeria fled for their home country, legitimately fearing retribution – Fanon had ominously stated in 1958 that '[t]he FLN finds itself justified today in calling into question not only the status of the French minority as it has conceived it up to now, but the very principle of existence of such a minority in the Algeria of tomorrow' (*AF* 598). The one-party state led by the FLN also forced leading Algerian leaders like the leftist Ahmed Ben Messali Hadj into exile and murdered supporters of rival factions. Independent Algeria was wracked by civil war between the government and Islamists, killing more people than those claimed by the French colonialist war. The political Islam that the FLN had strategically nurtured came back to bite them in the form of the Islamic Salvation Front (Front Islamique du Salut, FIS), a forerunner to organisations like the Taliban and the Muslim Brotherhood. One could say Fanon was lucky not to have witnessed this. His wife Josie Fanon committed suicide anguishing over the degeneration of an anti-colonial project into a savage and cynical struggle for power. The conflict, whose effects are felt till date, consumed the lives of progressive Algerian intellectuals like Tahar Djaout who was killed for refusing to comply with the diktats of the Islamist groups.

Fanon anticipated some, if not most, of this in *WOTE*. He warned against sectarianism, narrow identitarianism, nationalism and the ethnic hatred it could generate, one-party domination, personality cults, and the search for imagined authentic pasts. A careful reader could locate these apprehensions in his earlier works, *ADC* and *TAR,* both of which were written while he was a member of the FLN. Fanon, in the period, witnessed not only the everyday discriminations and humiliations that the Arabs faced, the terrible massacres committed by the French forces during counterinsurgency operations, but also the murder of dissidents by the FLN, most notably of his close friend and Algerian revolutionary Abane Ramdane who also belonged to the same group. Likewise, leaders, cadres and supporters of the leftist Algerian National Movement (Mouvement National Algérien, MNA) were also slaughtered by the FLN. After Ramdane's death, Fanon privately lamented, 'The Revolution is now in the hands of the goat herders' (Abane 42). While Fanon did not speak out against this publicly anywhere, a concern for the lack of intra-party democracy does appear in his last work. As a witness to a historical struggle, Fanon was aware that decolonisation was a violent affair, and also that violence scarred everyone who partook in it. But he did not want to accord himself the luxury of maintaining a comfortable distance – he regarded with much contempt French liberal intellectuals who condemned both sides in the war.

Fanon was a perennial outsider throughout his political life. He was a Black Martinician in white France, and later a French citizen in Africa, and one from a Christian background among Arab Muslims. Though he was fully committed to the Algerian anti-colonial struggle, he was never fully Algerian, and was never recognised as such. His influence on the course of the Algerian struggle was thin, save for his functioning as a useful intellectual face at solidarity conferences. Despite his illness in the last years of his life, Fanon was intensively involved in imparting political training to FLN cadres.

One of the texts which he frequently referred to was Sartre's *Critique of Dialectical Reason,* a work which, Fanon complained, was not given its due in France. One can legitimately wonder how much of it was taken seriously by the FLN. His grasp of pre-colonial Algerian history was hazy at best. Anti-Black racism among Arabs, Arab role in slavery, anti-Semitism in the Arab colonies and Islamic patriarchy were subjects he glossed over. Fanon's writings clearly show that his understanding of Islam as a socio-political factor in Algeria was superficial and he viewed it only in instrumental terms, vis a vis French colonialism. Cherki writes, 'While his political views never lost sight of the relationship between politics and culture, these were deeply rooted in atheism and the relationship between religion and politics never entered into them' (111). Fanon never subscribed to the idea that the Arab Muslim was the ideal citizen of Algeria, though this was the view held by many Algerian nationalists in the FLN. His notion of citizenship was based on secular premises. He would have been horrified to witness his appropriation by apologists for Islamism in recent times.

WOTE was an attempt at a systematic theorisation of a struggle for authentic decolonisation, and a forceful, passionate exhortation to achieve the same. Fanon was relying largely on the Algerian experience in *WOTE*, but he also referred to other movements in the African continent. While *WOTE* in time would become a manifesto for revolutionary movements, Fanon's contemporaries in the Third World were not particularly awed by it. For instance, Amílcar Cabral, the Marxist leader of Guinea-Bissau, was opposed to the romanticisation of the peasantry and the lumpen proletariat, while the Vietnamese Marxist Nguyen Nghe too decried Fanon's lack of understanding of the social classes in the anti-colonial revolution. However, Black militancy in the USA and the Anti-Apartheid movement in South Africa discovered *WOTE* as a weapon against oppression. The text that Fanon wrote primarily from his experiences in the Francophone Arab world would attain the status of a Bible for Black radicals in the Anglo-Saxon world. Much later, postcolonial studies would rediscover *BSWM* and proclaim it as the central text of Fanon. I, however, argue that a central theme that is common to all the texts of Fanon must be recovered. Fanon's words or texts cannot be read in isolation from one another, but must be seen systematically, as parts of a coherent theoretical whole. To have an understanding of Fanonism, and to use Fanonism to understand the world, neither the young Fanon of *BSWM* nor the old Fanon of *WOTE* must be privileged; a properly dialectical reading would trace the development of an essence, a theme, in his whole corpus.

READERS OF FANON NOW

In a world marked by grotesque economic inequalities and racial hostilities, Fanon will be passionately read by those who want to change the way things are. But for those who want to *interpret* the way things are – the act of interpreting itself is an act of changing – an apt question to ask would be *how* Fanon is relevant today. In *Fanon: A Critical Reader,* Lewis R. Gordon, T. Denean Sharpley-Whiting and Renee T. White identify five stages in Fanon studies (5–6). The first three stages involve applications of Fanon's works and reactions to it, biographical works on Fanon, and an assessment of Fanon's significance in political theory, in that order. The fourth stage 'linked to the ascent of postmodern cultural and postcolonial studies in the academy' includes, among others, the works of postcolonialists like Benita Parry, Edward Said and Homi Bhabha using Fanon. In the fifth stage Fanon is used as a tool, a method, a framework to study a variety of themes and issues. This stage works with and through Fanonism 'for the development of original work across the entire sphere of human studies. Its purpose is neither to glorify nor denigrate Fanon but instead to explore ways in which he is a useful thinker' (6–7). It can be said that this stage was formally inaugurated in the academia with the publication of *Fanon: A Critical Reader*. After this 'break', Fanonism has been used as a theoretical framework by many scholars to probe several contemporary social and political themes.

However, a minor criticism to this 'stages' approach can be made. Gordon et al. classify the 'stages' in Fanon studies in a linear, almost teleological, manner. But we can see that these stages often overlap and extend beyond their supposed time frames. For instance, for the first stage – that is, the 'practical' applications of and reactions to Fanon's thought – Gordon et al. list Fidel Castro, Che Guevara, Paulo Freire, Hannah Arendt, etc. To this list, from around that same time period, we can safely add Steve Biko, Malcolm X, Stokely Carmichael, activists of the Iranian revolution, the Palestinian struggle and so on. But Fanon is referenced by activists even today in their political strategies. Likewise, interest in Fanon's life and times also has not withered. Between 2014 and 2015 alone, there were four critical intellectual biographies on Frantz Fanon (Zeilig; Gordon; Lee; Hudis). Nevertheless, the idea of the five stages provides a broad blueprint of the manner in which Fanon has been read. I look at my own work as a contribution to the fifth stage, to read Fanon in a manner to understand the politics of identity and resistance today.

A general summary of the different ways in which Fanon has been used by postcolonialists has been provided in Henry Louis Gates Jr.'s popular essay 'Critical Fanonism'. Terming Fanon a 'Rashomon-like' character, a 'Rorschach blot on legs', Gates Jr. outlines the interpretations of Fanon by Homi Bhabha, Edward Said, Benita Parry and others. Disagreeing with Said, whom Gates Jr. accuses of attempting to frame Fanon as a global theorist, the essay concludes that reading Fanon requires an acknowledgement of his historical particularity and to not 'elevate him above his localities of discourse as a transcultural, transhistorical Global Theorist, nor simply to cast him into battle, but to recognize him as a battlefield in himself' (470).

To Edward Said, both Fanon and Césaire, 'jab directly at the question of identity and of identitarian thought, that secret sharer of present anthropological reflection on "otherness" and "difference"' (225). According to Said, both Fanon and Césaire required a rejection of fixed and culturally authorised definitions of identity. Benita Parry takes issue with Said's argument. Parry, citing Césaire and Fanon, argues that the task of postcolonial theory is 'to address the empowering effects of constructing a coherent identity or of cherishing and defending against calumniation altered and mutable indigenous forms, which is not the same as the hopeless attempt to locate and revive pristine pre-colonial culture' (179). Parry further suggests, in an explicit dig at Said, that 'the appointment of Fanon as exemplar of anticolonial theory liberated from identitarian thinking should be qualified' since his voyages into Negritude cannot be ignored (187).

It is interesting to note that some of those who have inferred a support for nativism in Fanon's writings have fallen back on Spivak's idea of 'strategic essentialism' to support themselves – while Spivak herself has claimed in the recent past that she has thoroughly repudiated that idea (260). Likewise, as a sort of a rejoinder to both Gates Jr. and Parry, Neil Lazarus, invoking Fanon, argues that '[f]rom the standpoint of postcolonialism, it is today impossible to think about politics without invoking the category of universality. For in the postcolonial world-system, experience is multiply overdetermined, and not least by imperialism itself. Social identity has become world-historical in its constitution' (219).

Of the various Indian postcolonialists who have engaged with Fanon, none can rival Homi Bhabha considering the passion with which he uses Fanon and the extent to which he has pushed Fanon in the broader postcolonial school. Bhabha is also the only academic to have written forewords to two books of Fanon, the 1986 Pluto Press edition of *BSWM* and the 2004 Grove Press edition of *WOTE*. Bhabha is well known for his use of the concept of 'mimicry' in understanding processes of identity formation under colonialism. Attributing the source of his arguments chiefly to Lacan and (a Lacanian version of) Fanon, he argues that 'colonial mimicry is the desire for a reformed, recognizable Other, as a subject of a difference that is almost the same, but not quite. Which is to say, that the discourse of mimicry is constructed around an ambivalence; in order to be effective, mimicry must continually produce its slippage, its excess, its difference' ('Of Mimicry and Man' 126). Bhabha uses Fanon as a tool to understand psychological (primarily) and political (secondarily) processes under colonialism. Bhabha implicitly privileges *BSWM* over *WOTE*, and the Lacan in Fanon over the Sartre in Fanon. The Fanon presented is an explorer of psycho-affective effects of colonialism. To Bhabha, Fanonian violence 'is part of a struggle for psycho-affective survival and a search for human agency in the midst of the agony of oppression' ('Framing Fanon' xxxvi). Bhabha gives a general overview of the (mis)appropriation of Fanon's arguments on violence by activists in identitarian movements across the world. He is right to assume that several of those who claim Fanon as an inspiration 'only absorb his abstract arguments and stirring sentiments' ('Framing Fanon' xxxi).

Bhabha, of course, has his critics. He has been accused of presenting a depoliticised Fanon. Where Gates Jr. faults Bhabha for promoting Fanon as a 'Third World post-structuralist' (465), Gibson faults him for divorcing Fanon from his global concerns. Gibson, who prefers an activist Fanon, challenges Bhabha's psychoanalyst Fanon. He argues that Bhabha's foreword to *WOTE* 'seems to be quite literally to judge Fanon's text, to subject the engaged intellectual to abstract (might I also say "bourgeois") moral judgments' ('Relative Opacity' 89). One could say in Bhabha's defence that he is not denying the potential use of Fanon by activists today, but is only seeking to problematise it. Bhabha's Fanon comes with problems, but he is definitely not a static historical figure.

A BRIEF COMMENT ON METHOD

One must not assume, however, that Fanon's works have any lesser relevance because postcolonial Algerian or African realities did not conform to the ideas expressed in these works. A very common error is to assume that a political thinker also plays the role of an astrologer and to fault them when results go contrary to their ideas. A great thinker's ideas cannot be judged in the contemporary on the sole basis of empirical realities, but rather on whether they might be useful in understanding reality today. The empirical fact that the Soviet Union collapsed does not make Marx irrelevant to understanding capitalism; atrocities against Dalits in Tamil Nadu cannot be cited as evidence to undermine Periyar's contributions to anti-caste thought. Likewise, the failure of the postcolonial project in Algeria and the sectarian warfare that followed independence do not diminish Fanonian perspectives on understanding identity and resistance. A rigorous theoretical critique cannot rely on pure historicism and relativist judgment. Rather, it has to look for tensions and possibilities within the works of a thinker. Reading Fanon today with the intention of *using Fanon today* must be more than a historicist study or a hermeneutic exercise. Fanon must be taken from the historical binary of colonialism/anti-colonialism and must be creatively read as a thinker for a different future.

Adorno begins his *Three Studies on Hegel* dismissing the question of Hegel's relevance. He asks instead 'what the present means in the face of Hegel' (1). When Fanon rather explicitly proclaimed in *BSWM* that 'I do not come with timeless truths' (1) and that 'I belong irreducibly to my time' (6), how can we legitimately and truthfully see our situation in his eyes? Conceding to Fanon (and to Bhabha), I agree that the *original truth* in Fanon's texts is irrevocably lost. Everything on Fanon *post-mortem* has only consisted of interpretations for specific political/social/academic projects and my work is no exception. But I also argue that it is possible to retain *fidelity* to the original texts of Fanon through an attempt to arrive at *truthful* readings by relying on the concepts and formulae used by Fanon in his texts and deciphering the essence of his works, and by a scrupulous avoidance of attributing ideas to Fanon that he had never written about. The last is a sin that quite a few readers of Fanon are guilty of. If such random interpretations are permitted, Fanon can easily be read as a lawyer for the Boko Haram and the ISIS. Anyone can be the interlocutor of a philosopher, Badiou said, 'But it is not true that any opinion is worth as much as any other opinion' (27). Fanon, the Rorschach blot, invites not only a variety of interlocutors but a bizarre assortment of interpretations and misinterpretations.

Criticising the 'mythology of doctrines' in the study of the history of ideas, Quentin Skinner says that the attempt to arrive at the fundamental thought or a coherent view of an author's system gives the thoughts of the author 'an air generally of a closed system, which they may have never aspired to attain' (68). But the understanding and the application of an *ism* like 'Fanonism' for theoretical study necessarily requires some form of systematisation. While it is necessary to avoid rigidity (a fundamental thought alone matters in the author's corpus), it is equally important to avoid excessive fluidity (the author's corpus has no fundamental thought in it). The former, of course, is totalitarianism. The latter, for lack of a better word, is nihilism. The quest, then, is for coherence in Fanon's corpus, through the study of the concepts he uses in his texts, the themes he addresses, and the pattern of his concerns. Umberto Eco defends the need to find a coherence in the texts of an author to avoid *overinterpretation* in that 'any interpretation given of a certain portion of a text can be accepted if it is confirmed by, and must be rejected if it is challenged by, another portion of the same text. In this sense the internal textual coherence controls the otherwise uncontrollable drives of the reader' ('Overinterpreting Texts' 65).

In his *Assorted Opinions and Maxims*, Nietzsche said that '[t]he worst readers are those who behave like plundering troops: they take away a few things they can use, dirty and confound the remainder, and revile the whole' (15–16). My effort is to avoid being such a reader of Fanon. This includes scrupulously avoiding the other 'mythology of doctrine' – that of 'converting some scattered or incidental remarks by a classic theorist into their "doctrine" on one of the expected themes' – and I also take heed of Skinner's warnings about the possibility of crediting the author with a meaning that he did not intend to convey or finding a personally preferred doctrine in the author's texts (60–61). I concur with Eco who asserts that '[t]o decide how a text works means to decide which one of its various aspects is or can become relevant or pertinent for a coherent interpretation of it, and which ones remain marginal and unable to support a coherent reading' ('Reply' 146). To this extent, I provide an outline of Fanon's humanism in the next chapter and on the basis of the same, seek to understand how he might be deployed to understand identity politics.

WHAT FOLLOWS

The next chapter, the key chapter of this book, provides a systematic theoretical outline of Fanon's humanism. I talk about Fanon's handling of the tensions between universality and particularity in identity politics and his assessment of the invocation of identity in racial and anti-colonial struggles. I argue that Fanon's political project was an aspiration towards a universalist human identity, which was in line with his adopted and adapted philosophy of Sartrean humanism. Sceptical of anti-colonial violence based only on cultural nationalism, and critical of racial and national particularism, Fanon made a compelling case for a struggle for reciprocal recognition, which would lead to mutual enriching of all cultures and peoples. Through shared solidarity and struggle against oppression and by replacing the false universality of the oppressor with a genuine universality of the oppressed, a new humanism would be born.

Following this, I explore Fanon's association with the literary-cultural movement of Negritude. I start with a discussion of Negritude, and how two main proponents of the idea, Léopold Senghor and Aimé Césaire, conceived it. The two thinkers were themselves not united in their vision of Negritude, except for the fact that they felt that a 'negro' identity deserved better recognition than what existed in Francophone societies. Jean-Paul Sartre's controversial introduction to an anthology of Negritude poetry, *Black Orpheus*, was and continues to be a subject of much debate. I seek to show how Fanon, contrary to the reading of many scholars, was more in line with Sartre's critique of Negritude; in fact, he was much harsher than Sartre in critiquing the pitfalls of this movement. Several Fanon scholars trace an explicit contradiction between Fanon and Sartre over the subject of Negritude. However, as I seek to prove, Fanon's engagement with Negritude was not one of simple positive appraisal, and correspondingly, his critique of Sartre's view on Negritude was not one of point-blank condemnation. Fanon, while unsparing in his condemnation of white racism, also noted the limits of the assertion of the Black identity. This fundamental Fanonist perspective helps us to look at identity politics elsewhere.

Fanon has been used to critically look at the politics of identity of whites, Blacks, Arabs, the indigenous, of Africanism, of nationalism, and even of gender. However, hitherto Fanon has never been used to read caste as a phenomenon. In the chapter titled 'Anti-Casteist Casteism? A Fanonist Study of Anti-Caste Politics',

I use the Fanonist perspective which I have developed in the earlier chapters to look at the anti-caste politics of a radical social reformer from south India, 'Periyar' E. V. Ramasamy (Periyar henceforth). A slightly different version of this chapter was published in *Interventions: International Journal of Postcolonial Studies* in 2017. Periyar was one of the most important, and controversial, anti-caste leaders in India in the twentieth century. A contemporary of leaders like B. R. Ambedkar and Mahatma Gandhi, Periyar is a household name in the south Indian state of Tamil Nadu and a key figure of Dravidian politics. Comparing and contrasting with Fanon's take on identity politics, I explore the limitations of Periyar's discursive strategies. Drawing a critique of Periyar from Fanon, I conclude that a transformative praxis in search of a post-casteist society must be based on a universalism that, while being cognisant of particulars, nevertheless unsettles both the identities of the oppressor and the oppressed. Reading Periyar's politics through Fanon, I not only provide a new way of looking at the anti-caste movement, but I also explore the possibilities of different ways of looking at identity *in* and *as* resistance.

A resistance movement based on identity can have self-imposed restrictions as well as radical possibilities. Almost mirroring each other, both identitarians and liberals focus only on the limiting, exclusivist aspects of identity politics, ignoring the other emancipatory aspects in it. A purely particularist approach to identification will take an identity as complete in itself – he is Black; she is white; they are Dalits; we are Tamils, etc. The politics of recognition and the politics of conflict that follows from such premises assume that individuals or groups must be respected/hated for the identity that they are born into. On the other hand, a critical universalist approach, a Fanonist approach, considers identification with an identity as what Jean-Luc Nancy would call metastable, 'never purely stable, nor simply plastic' (11), as something incomplete, with the possibility of becoming for-others. In the fifth chapter, I introduce and expand upon the idea of 'expansive identity' and why it is imperative for an ethical resistance movement. Here I discuss the Kurdish self-determination movement in West Asia as a case for the appreciation of the concept of expansive identity. Originating as a struggle for a separate Kurdish state in West Asia comprising territory that would cut into the geographies of Turkey, Syria, Iran and Iraq, the Kurdish movement under the leadership of the Kurdistan Workers Party (Partiya Karkerên Kurdistanê, PKK) eventually rejected nationalism and the idea of a nation state for the Kurds. Abdullah Öcalan, the key leader and theoretician of the Kurdish movement, proposes 'democratic confederalism' as an alternative to the centralised nation state, which he argues would provide 'an approach that weakens the capitalist modernity or pushes it back' (19). In *WOTE*, Fanon was apprehensive of the modern nation state in the newly liberated colonies and how nationalism might recede into ethnic chauvinism. Further, the significant role that the Kurdish movement allots to women as both leaders and fighters, and the centrality it places on women's autonomy is in stark contrast to the Algerian case and Fanon's reading of the same. Reading the Kurdish struggle with Fanon, I argue how identity assertion in resistance need not be exclusivist and solipsistic, but can be expansive, accommodative and *transfigurative*.

The conclusion deals with Fanonian readings of pop culture. I begin with a brief discussion of the phenomenon of interracial pornography, wherein racist and colonialist caricatures of Black bodies are turned into positive stereotypes, to cater to a fundamentally white fantasy of sexual transgression. I then discuss how the concept of identity was portrayed in successful Hollywood films like *Black Panther* (2018) and *X-Men: First Class* (2011), and how there is an increasing market for the marginal, and a fetishisation of identities. These forms of articulations of identities, actively encouraged by neo-liberal multiculturalism, make any forms of universal solidarities difficult, if not altogether impossible, even undesirable. Reading Fanon along with the works of contemporary philosopher Slavoj Žižek and political theorist Asad Haider's *Mistaken Identity* (2018), I discuss the implications of these trends for the politics of identity today, probing alternatives for a productive and progressive politics of resistance.

REFERENCES

Abane, Belaid. 'Frantz Fanon and Abane Ramdane: Brief Encounter in the Algerian Revolution'. *Living Fanon: Global Perspectives.* Ed. Nigel C. Gibson. New York: Palgrave Macmillan, 2011. 27–43. Print.

Adorno, Theodor W. *Hegel: Three Studies.* Trans. Shierry Weber Nicholsen. Cambridge: MIT Press, 1993. Print.

Arendt, Hannah. *On Violence.* New York: Harcourt Brace Jovanovich, 1969. Print.

Aubenas, Florence. 'In the Shadow of Frantz Fanon'. *Verso.* 21 November 2017. Web. 28 August 2018. < https://www.versobooks.com/blogs/3491-in-the-shadow-of-frantz-fanon>.

Badiou, Alain. *Philosophy for Militants.* Trans. Bruno Bosteels. London: Verso, 2012. Print.

Beauvoir, Simone de. *Force of Circumstance.* Trans. Richard Howard. Middlesex: Penguin, 1968. Print.

Bhabha, Homi K. 'Framing Fanon'. *The Wretched of the Earth.* By Frantz Fanon. Trans. Richard Philcox. New York: Grove Press, 2004. vii–xli. Print.

---. 'Of Mimicry and Man: The Ambivalence of Colonial Discourse'. *October* 28 (1984): 125–33. Print.

---. 'Remembering Fanon: Self, Psyche and the Colonial Condition'. *Black Skin, White Masks.* By Frantz Fanon. Trans. Charles Lam Markmann. London: Pluto Press, 2008. xxi–xxxvii. Print.

Cherki, Alice. *Frantz Fanon: A Portrait.* Trans. Nadia Benabid. New York: Cornell UP, 2006. Print.

Eco, Umberto. 'Overinterpreting Texts'. *Interpretation and Overinterpretation.* Ed. Stefan Collini. Cambridge: Cambridge UP, 1992. 45–66. Print.

---. 'Reply'. *Interpretation and Overinterpretation.* Ed. Stefan Collini. Cambridge: Cambridge UP, 1992. 139–41. Print.

Ehlen, Patrick. *Frantz Fanon: A Spiritual Biography.* New York: Crossroad Publishing Company, 2000. Print.

Fanon, Frantz. *A Dying Colonialism.* Trans. Haakon Chevalier. New York: Grove Press, 1965. Print.

---. *Alienation and Freedom.* Ed. Jean Khalfa, and Robert J. C. Young. Trans. Steven Corcoran. London: Bloomsbury, 2018. Print.

---. *Black Skin, White Masks.* Trans. Charles Lam Markmann. London: Pluto Press, 2008. Print.

---. *The Wretched of the Earth.* Trans. Richard Philcox. New York: Grove Press, 2004. Print.

---. *Toward the African Revolution: Political Essays.* Trans. Haakon Chevalier. New York: Grove Press, 1988. Print.

Gates Jr., Henry Louis. 'Critical Fanonism'. *Critical Inquiry* 17.3 (1991): 457–70. Print.

Gibson, Nigel C. *Fanon: The Postcolonial Imagination.* Cambridge: Polity, 2003. Print.

---. 'Relative Opacity: A New Translation of Fanon's *Wretched of the Earth*—Mission Betrayed or Fulfilled?'. *Social Identities: Journal for the Study of Race, Nation and Culture* 13.1 (2007): 69–95. Print.

Gordon, Lewis R. *What Fanon Said: A Philosophical Introduction to His Life and Thought.* London: Hurst & Company, 2015. Print.

Gordon , Lewis R., T. Denean Sharpley-Whiting, and Renee T. White. 'Introduction: Five Stages of Fanon Studies'. *Fanon: A Critical Reader.* Ed. Lewis R. Gordon, T. Denean Sharpley-Whiting, and Renee T. White. Oxford: Blackwell Publishers, 1996. 1–10. Print.

Haider, Asad. *Mistaken Identity: Race and Class in the Age of Trump.* London, New York: Verso, 2018. EPUB file.

Hudis, Peter. *Frantz Fanon: Philosopher of the Barricades.* London: Pluto Press, 2015. Print.

King Jr., Martin Luther. *The Autobiography of Martin Luther King, Jr.* Ed. Clayborne Carson. New York: Abacus, 2010. Print.

Lazarus, Neil. 'National Consciousness and the Specificity of (Post) Colonial Intellectualism'. *Colonial Dicourse/Postcolonial Theory.* Eds. Francis Barker, Peter Hulme, and Margaret Iversen. New York: Manchester UP, 1994. 197–220. Print.

Lee, Christopher J. *Frantz Fanon: Toward a Revolutionary Humanism.* Athens, OH: Ohio UP, 2015. Print.

Macey, David. *Frantz Fanon: A Life.* London: Granta Books, 2000. Print.

Manoharan, Karthick Ram. 'Anti-Casteist Casteism? A Fanonist Critique of Ramasamy's Discourse on Caste'. *Interventions*

19.1 (2017): 73–90. Print. https://doi.org/10.1080/1369801X.2016.1142885

Nancy, Jean-Luc. *Identity: Fragments, Frankness.* New York: Fordham UP, 2015. Print.

Nietzsche, Friedrich. *A Nietzsche Reader*. Ed. and Trans. R.J. Hollingdale. London: Penguin, 2003. Print.

Öcalan, Abdullah. *Democratic Confederalism.* Cologne: International Initiative, 2011. Print.

Parry, Benita. 'Resistance Theory/Theorising Resistance or Two Cheers for Nativism'. *Colonial Dicourse/Postcolonial Theory.* Eds. Francis Barker, Peter Hulme, and Margaret Iversen. New York: Manchester UP, 1994. 172–96. Print.

Said, Edward W. 'Representing the Colonized: Anthropology's Interlocutors'. *Critical Inquiry* 15.2 (Winter 1989): 205–25. Print.

Sartre, Jean-Paul. Preface. *The Wretched of the Earth*. By Frantz Fanon. Trans. Richard Philcox. New York: Grove Press, 2004. xliii–lxii. Print.

Skinner, Quentin. *Visions of Politics.* Cambridge: Cambridge UP, 2002. Print.

Spivak, Gayatri. *Other Asias.* Malden, MA: Blackwell Publishing, 2008. Print.

Williams, Robert R. *Recognition: Fichte and Hegel on the Other.* Albany: State U of New York P, 1992. Print.

Zeilig, Leo. *Frantz Fanon: The Militant Philosopher of Third World Revolution.* London: IB Tauris, 2014. Print.

Chapter Two

From Particular to Universal

THE CONTOURS OF FANON'S HUMANISM

> But in the very world, which is the world
> Of all of us,—the place where in the end
> We find our happiness, or not at all!
>
> William Wordsworth

This chapter seeks to provide an outline of Fanon's revolutionary humanism to enable the reader better understand his perspectives on the role of identity in resistance. It explores Fanon's critique of identity politics, and traces out its core aspects, to present how a transcendence of particularist identity to a universalist identity informed Fanon's views on the subject. The chapter begins with a discussion of identity and identity politics, engaging with poststructuralist, post-Marxist and liberal accounts of identity politics. Then it delves into Fanonian discussions of identity and identity politics. I begin with a discussion of the Master–Slave dialectic in Fanon, which was inspired by his reading of Alexandre Kojève's reading of Hegel. Following this, I talk about Fanon's handling of universality and particularity in identity politics, and I show how Fanon was interested in moving from particularism to a universalist humanism. The chapter argues that Fanon's identity project was about becoming human, which was in line with his philosophy of Sartrean humanism. Sceptical of cultural nationalism and racial and national particularism, Fanon placed his bet on a reciprocal recognition, which would lead to a mutual enriching of all cultures and peoples. Through shared solidarity and struggle against oppression and by replacing the false universality of the oppressor with a genuine universality of the oppressed, a new humanism would be born.

IDENTITY, IDENTIFICATION, IDENTITY POLITICS

According to Alexandre Kojève, a human being is self-conscious the moment she/he says 'I' (3). What is *I*? *I* is a person's sense of self at a particular time, in particular circumstances, which she/he shares in common with one set of people, and does not share with others. In short, *I* is the starting point of identity. Aristotle famously observed that to be aloof from society, one must be an animal or a god. One can make a similar observation about identity. Identity is always social. It is not possible for an individual to have an identity that is exclusive to her/him, that is uniquely personal and above society. When *I* claims an identity, it is always in relation to someone else. Or, *I* becomes and identity only when it has a sense of *we*. This is what William Connolly means when he says, 'Identity is *relational and collective*' (xiv; italics in original).

Bhikhu Parekh elucidates three types of identities – the personal, the social and the human. According to Parekh, personal identity defines individuals as 'unique human beings, distinct, as this person rather than some other', social identity 'pertains to their membership of different organizations, communities and structures of relationships . . . and leads to different forms and levels of social belonging', and human identity, 'the widest and also the shallowest, defines them simply as human beings' (28). While Parekh's definition of social identity is largely acceptable, his idea of personal identity is a bit too simplistic. As sociologist Richard Jenkins notes, 'Individual identity – embodied in selfhood – is not a meaningful proposition in isolation from the human world of other people. Individuals are unique and variable, but selfhood is thoroughly socially constructed' (18).

For instance, take 'Frantz Fanon'. As an individual who was born in Martinique in 1925 and who died in a hospital in Maryland in

1961, Frantz Fanon was a unique individual, just like the author of this book, or the reader of this book. And, unless one believes in a parallel universe, there was and will be only one Frantz Fanon. However, 'Frantz Fanon' is not an identity. Fanon possesses an identity by virtue of belonging to the Fanon family, a particular class, a particular nation, a particular gender, a particular sexual orientation, a particular political orientation, a particular literary preference, and so on. That is, Frantz Fanon has an identity, or as Parekh would have it, a social identity, only by virtue of belonging to a social group. Frantz Fanon, by himself, is not a Black, a French Martinician, or even a man or a human – all of these are identities conferred on him by discursive practices, which he accepts, or rejects, or refashions according to his agency.

In his account of identity and agency, cultural theorist Stuart Hall, taking from Michel Foucault, argues that what is to be considered is not a theory of subjectivity but rather that of discursive practices. He qualifies that this is an attempt 'to rearticulate the relationship between subjects and discursive practices that the question of identity recurs – or rather, if one prefers to stress the process of subjectification to discursive practices, and the politics of exclusion which all such subjectification appears to entail, the question of *identification*' (2). What is to be noted here is that Hall relatively privileges discursive practices in the construction of identity over the subjectivity of the actor. As I will argue later, to Fanon, it is ultimately agency that counts.

To Hall, identification is never complete, never a totality or a subsumption, but rather a suturing (3). David Howarth also lays emphasis on a shift from identity to identification. In the process of identification, political frontiers are produced 'by complicated hegemonic practices which divide social spaces and confer identity by creating antagonistic relations between forces, and by linking together different demands and subjectivities into common projects' (243). Here we see a marked progression from identity to identity politics. Or, we can say that identity politics begins for the individual when the *I* begins a process of identification with an identity *as different from and as opposed to* another identity/identities.

I enters the realm of the political when it is part of a *we* and recognises an oppositional *they*. Opposition and conflict are central to the Fanonist conception of identity politics, as we shall see.

However, the liberal camp is likely to take offense at this position. For instance, to Amartya Sen, plurality of identities at any given point in time must be acknowledged and respected, and he opposes the 'singular affiliation' to any particular identity. He argues, 'The incitement to ignore all affiliation and loyalties other than those emanating from one restrictive identity can be deeply delusive and also contribute to social tension and violence' (21). In Sen's perspective, an individual's identity as a football fan is as important as her identity as a woman from a particular social, ethnic or national group. What Sen, in essence, is advocating is a liberal politics of *apolitical* recognition where individuals recognise the plurality of identities of their self and of others without identification with any particular identity and avoiding social antagonisms – thus avoiding politics itself. This is fine under conditions of absolute peace. In situations where the existing system has thrust an identity upon a group against its consent, an inferiorised identity like that of the Blacks in the US or the backward castes in India, or follows a policy of forcible assimilation like in the case of the Tamils in Sri Lanka or the Kurds in Turkey, the true political act is to not just recognise pluralities, but to suture a unity from these pluralities, an identification, a hegemonic process, to bring together 'different demands and subjectivities into common projects', to take from Howarth above.

Sen misses the difference between roles and identities. According to sociologist Manuel Castells, roles 'are defined by norms structured by the institutions and organizations of society' whereas identities are 'people's source of meaning and experience' and provide a stronger source of meaning than roles 'because of the process of self-construction and individuation that they involve' (7). Castells also introduces three types of identity – namely, legitimising identity 'introduced by the dominant institutions of society to extend and rationalize their domination *vis a vis* social actors'; resistance identity 'generated by those actors who are in positions/conditions devalued and/or stigmatized by the logic of domination, thus building trenches of resistance and survival on the basis of principles different from, or opposed to, those permeating the institutions of society'; and project identity 'when social actors, on the basis of whatever cultural materials are available to them, build a new identity that redefines their position in society and, by so doing, seek the transformation of overall social structure' (8). These three types will be of use to understand Fanon's conceptualisation of identity politics.

In general, identity politics has been a subject of scorn by leftists for reducing politics to narrow particularities which make any form of larger emancipatory movements impossible. Likewise, it has been defended by postmodernists for being a celebration of diversity and multiculturalism. Avoiding both extremes, I seek to show, with Fanon, how an emancipatory politics of identity necessarily entails identification with an identity which also has the potential to transcend itself into something larger. This takes from Ernesto Laclau's observation that '[t]here is no politics of pure particularity. Even the most particularistic of demands will be made in terms of something transcending it' (305).

Following are the questions that I seek to address in this chapter: What is the Fanonist conception of identity politics? What are the normative contours it is shaped by? How are the tensions between the particular and the universal resolved? And, finally, is the 'human identity' of Parekh an 'identity project' for Fanon?

IDENTITY AND THE MASTER–SLAVE DIALECTIC IN FANON

Fanon explicitly addresses the Hegelian theme of recognition – that is, the dialectic of the Master and the Slave – in *BSWM*. Fanon scholar Hussein Bulhan notes that Fanon, like Sartre, was influenced by Kojève's interpretations of Hegel (102). According to Kojève, to recognise the Other without being recognised by her/him is the basis of Hegelian schemata of the Master–Slave dialectic (8). In the beginning of the dialectical process, the Master is in a privileged status, because by virtue of force and violence, she/he has been recognised by the Slave. The Master's humanity is recognised as universal and absolute. Likewise, the Master's humanity necessarily rests on a progressive dehumanisation of the Slave. That is, 'the Master is Master only by the fact of having a Slave who recognizes him as Master' (Kojève 8).

The Slave works for the Master without being recognised. Yet, it is through this work that the seeds of self-consciousness are sown. And if at all the Slave needs recognition, she/he needs to risk her/his life and overcome the fear of death through a fight with the Master. Since the Master has laid claim to universality by virtue of domination, the Slave, through the fight, seeks the recognition of her/his particularity *in* an abstract universality. That is to say, 'He is not content with attributing a value to himself. He wants this particular value, *his own,* to be recognized by *all* men, *universally*' (Kojève 58; italics in original).

Fanon echoes this when he says, 'He who is reluctant to recognize me opposes me. In a savage struggle I am willing to accept convulsions of death, invincible dissolution, but also the possibility of the impossible' (*BSWM* 170). But what Fanon is talking about here is not a plea for multicultural tolerance or fair treatment by the law. Hudis rightly notes that '[r]ecognition, for Hegel as well as for Fanon, is about much more than acknowledging an individual's formal equality before the law: it is instead a demand to be recognized for the dignity and worth of one's being' (4). But what complicates Fanon's perspective is that he takes Hegel a step further, and contextualises Hegel with respect to the Black racial situation by adding the dimension of the coloured Slave. Hudis convincingly argues that 'Fanon departs from Hegel in denying that the black slave necessarily achieves an independent self-consciousness through his work, but in doing so he is in accord with Hegel's broader view that the struggle for recognition is not resolved at the rather provisional stage of the master/slave dialectic' (5). With a Sartrean analysis, Fanon notes that the Black is created by the gaze of the white. The white person, who possessed material superiority, also possessed an epistemological superiority which gave her/him power not just to make the Slave work for the Master's interests but also to define the Slave as 'Black', to determine the paradigms of discourse under which the Slave's identity was structured. That is, epistemological superiority was a precursor to create discursive practices that constructed an epidermal superiority.

Thus, the white identity, 'whiteness', is the standard towards which the Black aspires. In this 'world of becoming' in a society characterised by unequal relationships between racially marked social groups, for the Black, becoming white means becoming more human. While the white is recognised without recognising in return, it is the Black who needs recognition from the white, and this is why Fanon claims that the Black undergoes a process of 'lactification'. The desire of the woman of colour for the white man and the desire of the man of colour for the white woman are but manifestations of the desire to be more human in a world where whiteness is the norm. The white identity is the legitimising identity which the Master wields by virtue of her/his material and epistemological power. Even when the white colonial Master talks about man or humanity, she/he is referring only to her/his own image. Even when the white Master frees the coloured Slave and abolishes the material conditions of slavery, the unequal relationship persists because, to Fanon, the 'Negro Slave' is one who has *not* fought or risked her/his life for freedom. 'Historically, the Negro steeped in the inessentiality of servitude was set free by his master. He did not fight for his freedom' (*BSWM* 170).

The Black was given 'freedom' as a gift by the white Master and it mutilated the process of reciprocal recognition, because mere 'recognition' in a colonial context does nothing to alter the living condition, both economic and psychic, of the Black. Since there was no fight proper, she/he seeks to either further mutilate herself/himself by imitating the white Master, or enter into the particularist solipsism of Negritude. Without an ethical recognition, the Black is torn between the myth of a superior white humanity and the myth of a pristine and pure Black past. The politics of Black experience, for all its claims to separatism, was still functioning in the discursive paradigms set by the whites. A Hegelian insight is useful here, 'The one who flees, however, is not yet free, for in fleeing he is still dependent on what he flees' (Hegel 149). As Jenkins observes, 'The capacity of authoritatively applied identification to constitute or influence individual experience affects whether or not individuals internalise the label(s) concerned' (20).

To Fanon, both white liberalism and Black identitarianism are just attempts to reform the system. The man who does not/has not experienced the fear of death and waged a fight to the death for recognition is bound to the existing world and at best, only attempts to reform it 'to change its details, to make particular transformations without modifying its essential characteristics' – but considering that the given world is the world of the Master and the Master's version of humanity or universality, 'it is not reform, but the "dialectical", or better, revolutionary overcoming of the World that can free him and – consequently – satisfy him' (Kojève 29). In Fanon's view, both assimilating into the white culture and romanticising a Black past were mere reformist attempts and not a radical rupture with the status quo.

To some extent, Negritude could be called a politics of resistance identity because it contests the inferior status conferred on to the Blacks by the whites in power, and calls on the Blacks to take pride in their selves. Its 'anti-racist racism' and belief in the uniqueness of Black particularity could be explained as '*the exclusion of the excluders by the excluded*' (Castells 9; italics in original). However, to Fanon, it still was, to take from Sartre, a passing phase in the dialectic and not an end in itself. A pitfall of Negritude was that in its attempts to reject white racist definitions, it overidentified with an imagined Negro authenticity and Negro pasts, leading Fanon to comment that 'Negro' was only a cultural term that had no historical or sociological basis (*TAR* 17). Further, he writes, 'When one says "Negro people," one systematically assumes that all Negroes agree on certain things, that they share a principle of communion. The truth is that there is nothing, *a priori,* to warrant the assumption that such a thing as a Negro people exists' (18). We will discuss Fanon's critique of Negritude in greater detail in the next chapter.

An identity, to Fanon, cannot conjure up mythical and pristine pasts but must be historicised. Likewise, a politics that emanates from it must not be based on unique communal experiences of the past but with a vision for the future. This is why Fanon begins the conclusion of *BSWM* with a quote from Karl Marx's *The Eighteenth*

Brumaire of Louis Bonaparte: 'The social revolution . . . cannot draw its poetry from the past, but only from the future. It cannot begin with itself before it has stripped itself of all its superstitions concerning the past' (174). To overcome the Master–Slave dialectic that existed in the white–Black relationships, the whole of the past had to be set aside in the interests of a common future where human beings would be recognised as human beings. Both the whites and Blacks 'must turn their backs on the inhuman voices which were those of their respective ancestors in order that authentic communication be possible' (*BSWM* 43).

Fanon's consternation with Negritude is owing to its excessive emphasis on the uniqueness of the Black identity and experience which only assists compartmentalisation of peoples and not a resolution of the conflict. The Slave does resist the Master's values but without providing a value that would overcome the relationship of difference. The prejudice of the Black towards her/his own race was not a path to universal political liberation but only an abstract cultural dialogue that only her/his own hear. Whereas, Fanon argues, 'A people that undertakes a struggle for liberation rarely legitimizes race prejudice' (*TAR* 43). In a sense, Fanon anticipates the contemporary debates around 'reverse racism' and empathetically states his opposition to any sort of racial essentialism. In his very first book, Fanon places his lot on the side of a universalist humanism that he uses as an evaluating standard in his assessment of identity politics. Sonia Kruks is thus right to argue that while Fanon believed that to affirm, express, or celebrate one's identity can be psychologically empowering, he ultimately was of the opinion that affirmation of identity alone was not enough to change the world (Kruks 133).

Fanon's identity politics needed more than a relic of the past, 'a black mirage', to validate itself. This leads to the question of identification. Now, we can see that Fanon was strongly sceptical of identification with an essentialised, valorised racial identity that claimed validation only through particularity and lived experience. It is in positing an alternative to this – as well as to the white colonial racism that marks itself as the universal face of humanity – that the

Fanonian tensions between universality and particularity emerge. It is necessary to understand Fanon's critical assessment of this problem in order to arrive at a clear picture of the norms that guided his position on identity politics.

FANON, UNIVERSALITY AND PARTICULARITY

Commenting on Fanon's relationship with 'Negritude', Benita Parry writes that 'Fanon's writings function at a point of tension between cultural nationalism and transnationality, without "resolving" the contradiction and without yielding an attachment to the one or the aspiration to the other' (187). Though Parry is generally in favour of the resistance identity of Negritude, she concedes that Fanon, in opposing both the nativism of Negritude and the idealism of European humanism, was 'projecting the radical hope of an oppositional humanism' (193). This 'oppositional humanism' of Fanon, which reveals the fallacies of the narrow particularities of Negritude and the hypocrisies of European humanism, constitutes Fanon's identity project.

We can see that throughout his works Fanon operates with a Sartrean understanding that '*Particularism* can and must claim the status of *universality* in the absence of a comprehensive frame of reference, since to be in perspective necessarily transforms particularism itself into its *own perspective,* and thus into the measure of everything else' (Meszaros 13; italics in original). In *BSWM,* the essays on 'West Indians and Africans' and 'Racism and Culture' in *TAR*, and his chapter on 'The Pitfalls of National Consciousness' in *WOTE,* Fanon deploys mock sarcasm against those among the Blacks and the colonised who focus only on racial and/or national particularities without taking the next step towards universality. Likewise, he also targets the humanism of Europe for being a facade for imperialism and suggests a new revolutionary humanism in its place. How does Fanon make the transition from particularity to universality?

It is necessary to have a grasp of the essence of the whole corpus of Fanon's works in order to understand how he negotiates the tensions between universality and particularity. In *BSWM*, Fanon addresses the problem of Black identity in a Francophone scenario, mainly in the Antilles and in France. He states his goal clearly at the outset – 'Toward a new humanism' (1). This new humanism is necessary because '[t]he white man is sealed in his whiteness' and '[t]he black man in his blackness' (3). According to Robert Bernasconi,

> Fanon never lost sight of the fact that historically the discussion of race has always been under the sway of racism and that, if we continue to talk about race, it should only be because the struggle against racism is far from over and that the concept of race, employed properly, was a vital tool in combating racism. . . . He insisted that the struggle should be conducted under the auspices of an attempt to create a new way of thinking and a new humanity. (85–86)

That is, the discussions of the particularity of race must always give way to a synthesis of a common humanity where colour would cease to be a factor in assessing an individual's worth. Fanon was compelled to discuss the pathology of white racism and the Black reaction to it, the 'anti-racist racism' of Negritude, so as to arrive at a common and new humanism. Fanon's first book is not so much about the colonial encounter as his later works were, though the scenario of colonialism clearly looms in the background. In a society that is racist, that racially privileges one group over the other, 'The feeling of inferiority of the colonized is the correlative to the European's feeling of superiority. . . . *It is the racist who creates his inferior*' (*BSWM* 69; italics in original). While he takes inspiration from Sartre's thesis that the anti-Semite invents the Jew (Sartre, *Anti-Semite and Jew* 13), Fanon places greater focus on the agency of the 'inferior' to create her/his own identification in a situation of oppression. Or, the Black person, though 'overdetermined from without' by a racist society and who is a slave of his own appearance (*BSWM* 87), is nevertheless free to choose who she/he identifies with and how she/he frames her/his politics.

The subject, though identified by others as a 'Negro', still has the choice of choosing her/his own identification. However, Fanon's humanism, which he derives greatly from Sartre, is not a liberal concept of individual choice or self-discovery, because one not only discovers one's own self (as say, a Black or a white) but others' as well – a woman/man cannot be anything unless the others recognise her/him as such (Sartre, *Existentialism and Humanism* 45). On this, Sartre elaborates,

> I cannot obtain any truth whatsoever about myself, except through the mediation of another. The other is indispensible to my existence, and equally so to any knowledge I can have of myself. Under these conditions, the intimate discovery of myself is at the same time the revelation of the other as freedom which confronts mine, and which cannot think or will without doing so either for or against me. (45)

The Black person's discovery of her/his self confronts the agency of the white who, privileged by the system, refuses an ethical recognition of the former. The white who does not recognise the Black opposes the Black, and the Black must wage a fight to attain this recognition. But recognitions as what? To Fanon, the person neither 'has the right to be a Negro' nor 'the duty to be this or that', but if the white challenges his humanity, the racialised individual must impose his 'whole weight as a man' on the white and check, challenge and change the oppressor's prejudices (*BSWM* 178). To Fanon, thus, the individual has one right – 'That of demanding human behavior from the other' – and one duty – 'That of not renouncing my freedom through my choices' (179). And this radically free subject cannot search for her/his destiny in history but rather in a common future. This is the essence of the Hegelian idea of recognition: 'If recognition occurs, it must occur through the mutual and joint action of both, through which the "I's" become a "We"' (Williams 157).

This is why Fanon is deeply sceptical about projects that focus more on particularist pasts than on a common future. He says, 'The discovery of the existence of a Negro civilization in the fifteenth century confers no patent of humanity on me. Like it or not, the past can in no way guide me in the present moment' (*BSWM* 176). The Black should not be locked up into her/his particularist identity and must make a movement towards something larger. When Fanon claims in the last chapter of *BSWM* that it is not the particular history of 'Negro civilization' but the entire history of human civilisation that interests him, he also adds that 'The body of history does not determine a single one of my actions' (*BSWM* 180). Fanon places the onus on the individual's agency in deciding what their identity is, what their identification is, and what their identity politics will be. Here, he echoes the Sartrean humanist thought of radical subjectivity that '[m]an is nothing else but that which he makes of himself' (Sartre, *Existentialism and Humanism* 28).

Fanon speaks more of this in his later writings: 'It is the white man who creates the Negro. But it is the Negro who creates negritude' (*ADC* 47). That is, though the particular identity of the Negro might have been created by the white-colonial-Other, it is the subjectivity of the colonised that creates identification with Negritude. After criticising the particularist politics of Negritude for depriving the Blacks of 'any possibility of individual expression' (*TAR* 17), Fanon makes explicit what to him constitutes a genuine universalist humanism: 'universality resides in this decision to recognize and accept the reciprocal relativism of different cultures once the colonial status is irreversibly excluded' (*TAR* 44).

Two things need to be noted here. First, the end of colonialism as a system is an unconditional and preliminary step to an ethical recognition among peoples. In all his works, Fanon is uncompromising in his belief that colonialism is an absolute evil and that the colonised is psychologically conditioned to rejecting the values of the occupier 'even if these values objectively be worth choosing' (*ADC* 63). The humanity of the colonised 'can only materialize from the rotting cadaver of the colonist' (*WOTE* 50). He qualifies that '[a]t the individual level, violence is a cleansing force. It rids the colonized of their inferiority complex, of their passive and despairing attitude. It emboldens them, and restores their self-confidence' (*WOTE* 51). Violence is an act of self-affirmation in the quest for an ethical recognition where that recognition has been denied to the colonised. Colonialism as a system deprives the colonised of their self-worth. The native culture is devalued, mutilated and criminalised while that of the coloniser is elevated as a model for emulation, and imposed on the natives. To Fanon, in the colonial apparatus, the colonialist projects himself as the image of humanity while concurrently denying the humanity of the colonised. It was Fanon's uncompromising belief that 'authentic decolonization is irreconcilable with anything that colonialism stands for, because colonialism is essentially a negation of the identity of the colonized' (Onwuanibe 109). It is only through ending this system and the physical ejection of the coloniser that the humanity of the colonised could be realised and the transition to universalism could be made. Real universal humanism for Fanon begins after the elimination of the colonial Other, the Enemy.

Second, reciprocal recognition and acceptance of the relativism of cultures provide an ethical premise for universalism. According to Adele Jinadu, Fanon's ethical relativism is a form of cultural relativism, which rejects the universality of the colonising country (149). Likewise, Pramod Nayar argues that Fanon's ethical recognition requires recognising the identity of all Others, a mutuality of recognition, respecting difference without erasing or homogenising it (123). However, it must be added that Fanon is careful about unqualified cultural relativism, as he makes clear in his discussions about Negritude or about the 'Trials and Tribulations of National Consciousness' in *WOTE*, wherein he prefers a switch from national consciousness to a social and political consciousness (*WOTE* 142) and for nationalism to be 'explained, enriched and deepened' and to be elevated into humanism (144). Anti-colonialism was not an end in itself. It was a means to an end, an absolutely necessary means albeit.

Fanon believes in what Slavoj Žižek calls 'universality-for-itself'. According to Žižek, 'The universality-for-itself is not simply external to or above its particular context: it is inscribed within it. It perturbs and affects it from within, so that the identity of the particular is split into its particular and universal aspects' (129). Fanon's universalism emerges from his deep commitment to anti-colonial resistance and decolonisation. But while there is a general valorisation of the anti-colonial aspects of Fanon's writings, scholars often overlook Fanon's concern about how the former colony fares after decolonisation in its humanising project. Which is why in 'This Africa to Come', Fanon states explicitly that '[c]olonialism and its derivatives do not, as a matter of fact, constitute the present enemies of Africa. In a short time this continent will be liberated.

For my part, the deeper I enter into the cultures and the political circles the surer I am that the great danger that threatens Africa is the absence of ideology' (*TAR* 186).

While the moment of colonial encounter is crucially important in shaping the identity of the colonised and her/his identification with a national project of decolonisation, it alone does not justify a politics of the future. To Fanon, such a politics would have to transform not just the identity of the oppressed, but also that of the oppressor. Given that the ideology of the European colonialist, despite its claims to universal humanism, functions in practice as 'nothing but a dishonest ideology, an exquisite justification for plundering' (Sartre, Preface lviii), it was necessary for the colonised to take up this mission – 'For Europe, for ourselves and for humanity, comrades, we must make a new start, develop a new way of thinking, and endeavor to create a new man' (Fanon, *WOTE* 239).

BECOMING HUMAN: FANON'S IDENTITY PROJECT

It is instructive here to consider what Laclau would term a discursive strategy of hegemonic articulation: 'there is hegemony only if the dichotomy universality/particularity is superseded; universality exists only incarnated in – and subverting – some particularity but, conversely, no particularity can become political without becoming the locus of universalizing effects' (Laclau, 'Identity and Hegemony' 56). Fanon deals with this paradox throughout his writings. His concerns with race, colonialism and anti-colonial nationalism are the particularities in which the possibility of a universalist humanism is incarnated, and, likewise, these particularities are to be transcended to arrive at this universalism. Fanon, in arriving at his identity project, is neither taking a Marxist approach that reduces the individual to structures, nor does he take an approach which ignores structures and focuses purely on choice. Fanon's identity project of becoming human evolves from a Sartrean understanding of dialectic that '[m]an undergoes the dialectic, in so far as he makes it, and makes it, in so far as he undergoes it. He is not subject to it non-dialectically, like a divine law, or a metaphysical fatality: and it does not emanate from himself non-dialectically, as though he were its unconditioned creator' (Laing and Cooper 100).

Or, humans have the capacity to make something out of themselves from within the limits set by circumstances, recognising these limits and pushing towards a transcendence of these limits. To Fanon, the object of all societies based on oppression – be they of racism, or class, or colonialism – is to dehumanise one set of people for the benefit of others. The oppressed subject reacts to the oppressive system through broadly three ways – acceptance and assimilation, *overidentification* with an inferiorised identity (Negritude) and a consequent valorisation of the same, and creation of an emancipatory ideology of resistance that would transform both oppressor and oppressed and replace the oppressive system with one that is universally just.

So, to Fanon, violent resistance of the oppressed is merely instrumental in ending a system of structural violence. Liberal critics of Fanon, like Arendt who alleges that he 'glorified violence for violence's sake' (65), are thus missing this crucial point. The criticism that Žižek lays at those whom he sarcastically terms 'liberal communists' (31) can also be laid at such critics of Fanon – while they condemn the subjective violence that Fanon (allegedly) celebrates, they overlook the fact that this subjective violence is a product of, and is intended to end, a structural violence. While he was deeply aware of the negative psychological implications of subjective violence on the colonised as is evident in his chapter on 'Colonial War and Mental Disorders' in *WOTE,* Fanon's primary concern was to end the structural violence of colonialism which to him was far more insidious. He anticipates Johan Galtung who, in his widely cited essay on violence, argues that '[p]ersonal violence represents change and dynamism – not only ripples on waves, but waves on otherwise tranquil waters. Structural violence is silent, it does not show – it is essentially static, it *is* the tranquil waters' (173; italics in original). To Fanon, anti-colonial violence was a dynamic force that would sharpen the political resolve of the natives and violate the tranquillity of not just the colonial power, but also that of the native elite.

Thus, 'Anticolonialism is not the end; it must be filled out and developed into a practice and awareness of political and social inclusion of the most marginal, and only then will it have developed into a true humanism' (Gibson 9). Fanon considers anti-colonialism as a necessary and strategic political tool to move towards his identity project. As Lee observes, 'Decolonization only marked a political end point. It still remained a starting point for remaking humankind' (153). Once the 'primary contradiction', to use a Maoist term, of coloniser–colonised is resolved, the erstwhile colonised has to face the native elite or the comprador class which prevents them from fully achieving their humanity. This class uses the narrative of a narrow nationalism to legitimise its own privilege to the detriment of the impoverished, often aiding neocolonialism in the process. In the postcolony, this elite is the new enemy of the people and the 'manicheist classification of black and white' disappears and the masses recognise that '[o]ne is deprived or privileged in virtue of one's economic and social association' (Jean-Marie 117).

Fanon notes how the landowners and the urban bourgeoisie in an underdeveloped newly decolonised country ensure that 'development' favours only their sectarian interests – under this bourgeoisie that is both selfish and incompetent, anti-colonialism quickly gives way to racism and chauvinism (Fanon, *WOTE* 103). While the racism of the European colonialist is fuelled by contempt, the racism of the young urban national bourgeoisie is fuelled by fear (110). With neither the extensive resources nor the expertise of the erstwhile Master, the new bourgeoisie resorts to crude methods of force, simultaneously justifying its own status through appeals to a mythical past and narrow nationalism. This is why Fanon places his lot among the peasantry, whom he considers the most affected by colonial political economy, and is deeply suspicious of both the urban bourgeoisie and the proletariat. To him, both were privileged by the colonial apparatus and must be checked by a vigilant activism of the peasantry, if at all there is to be an equitable distribution of resources in the postcolony. In such countries, 'the combined efforts of the masses, regimented by a party and of keenly conscious intellectuals, armed with revolutionary principles, should bar the way to this useless and harmful bourgeoisie' (119).

These intellectuals, who are in an organic relation with the masses, will create a national culture. But this is a culture that is not purely based on customs, traditions and artefacts of the past, but 'the values that inspired the struggle for freedom' (Fanon, *WOTE* 179). The activist–intellectual uses the resources of the past selectively through the evaluating standard of the anti-colonial struggle, and projects them onto the future of the nation as a national culture. But this national culture, rather than emphasising differences among people, attempts to foster a spirit of shared solidarity. Scholars have called this Fanonian outlook 'nationalitarian', as a concept that is different from and opposed to bourgeois nationalism (Lazarus 199). This was the resistance identity that he preferred to the racial categories of Negritude. Fanon calls for dismantling 'not only the racial binaries of colonialism *but also* the xenophobic cultural nationalism of postcolonial nations' (Nayar 128; italics in original). In his vision, bourgeois cultural nationalism in decolonised countries was not just undesirable but it was also dangerous because of its inability to maintain hegemony over the new country. This would inevitably lead to factions and feuds, and foster sectarian violence in the postcolony, only to benefit neocolonial forces that would seek to keep their exploitative economic relations with their former colonies intact.

While one of Fanon's immediate goals was African unity, 'a principle on the basis of which it is proposed to achieve the United States of Africa without passing through the middle-class chauvinistic national phase' (Fanon, *TAR* 187), his eventual goal was a solidarity among the oppressed of the world which would enable them in a revolutionary restructuring of society. Yet, Fanon is also concerned about the erstwhile oppressor. It must be realised that Fanon does not criticise Europe for being Europe – he criticises it for not being Europe *enough*. 'All the elements for a solution to the major problems of humanity existed at one time or another in European thought. But the Europeans did not act on the mission that was designated them' (*WOTE* 137). These words are a lament, not a curse. The Third World must transform itself *for itself* and also *for Europe* and *for a new humanism*. So, Sartre's message to European readers in his preface to *WOTE* that 'Fanon has got nothing "in for you" at all' (xlv) must be treated as hyperbole.

Fanon's idea of identity politics seeks to transform the identities of both the oppressor and the oppressed, encouraging them to transcend closures. He does not want to replace anti-Black hatred with anti-white hatred, but urges to banish all forms of racism and oppression and to 'work for man, for the flourishing of man and for the enrichment of humanity' (*AF* 657). His need to 'to explain the other to myself' (*BSWM* 181) is infused with a radical hope of the Self and the Other mitigating their particularities and eventually merging, maybe with the instrumental use of violence, to alter the system that maintains these narrow particularities, into a 'We'. This was Fanon's 'identity project' – a human identity in a 'world of all of us'.

CONCLUSION

From the above study, the contours of Fanon's humanism can be traced. One, the individual is fully free in identifying with an identity despite the limits that circumstances place upon her/him. The oppressed have an agency and thereby responsibility in fashioning their identity politics of the future from the resources that they can avail of from their historical context.

Two, anti-colonialism was absolutely necessary for an emancipatory political project and identification of the colonised with the anti-colonial resistance was a necessary step. Since European humanism failed to realise its emancipatory potential and served instead as a mask for colonial domination, it had to be rejected, and the oppressed could not achieve anything progressive in the colonial setup. The perpetuation of colonialism would only mutilate the identity of the colonised, whereas resistance to it, and identification with the resistance, opens up liberating possibilities.

Three, while cultural differences should be recognised reciprocally in a spirit of conditional relativism, racial or national particularism always has pitfalls. After the end of the colonial status, which is a non-negotiable condition for a politics of the future, the colonised nevertheless realise that the coloniser is not the only oppressor, and that the oppressor within can be as brutal as the oppressor without and that they can also mobilise the legacy of anti-colonial nationalism to further their own benefits. Therefore, while anti-colonialism is absolutely necessary, there should also be a conscious ideological attempt to transcend nationalism.

Four, the transcendence of a particular social identity of race and nation must arrive at a universal human identity. Shared solidarity and struggle against oppressions are necessary to arrive at this universalism. In the spirit of his revolutionary humanism, Fanon advocates a counter-universalism, wherein he rejects the false universalism of the coloniser to replace it with a universalism of the oppressed, which alone would be a true universalism.

REFERENCES

Arendt, Hannah. *On Violence*. New York: Harvest/HBJ, 1970. Print.

Bernasconi, Robert. 'The Great White Error and the Great Black Mirage: Frantz Fanon's Critical Philosophy of Race'. *Living Fanon: Global Perspectives*. Ed. Nigel Gibson. New York: Palgrave Macmillan, 2011. 85–92. Print.

Bulhan, Hussein Abdilahi. *Frantz Fanon and the Psychology of Oppression*. New York: Plenum Press, 1985. Print.

Castells, Manuel. *The Power of Identity*. 2nd ed. West Sussex: Wiley-Blackwell, 2010. Print.

Connolly, William E. *Identity/Difference: Democratic Negotiations of Political Paradox*. Expanded ed. Minnesota: U of Minnesota P, 1991. Print.

Fanon, Frantz. *A Dying Colonialism*. Trans. Haakon Chevalier. New York: Grove Press, 1965. Print.

---. *Alienation and Freedom*. Eds. Jean Khalfa and Robert J. C. Young. Trans. Steven Corcoran. London: Bloomsbury, 2018. Print.

---. *Black Skin, White Masks*. Trans. Charles Lam Markmann. London: Pluto Press, 2008. Print.

---. *The Wretched of the Earth*. Trans. Richard Philcox. New York: Grove Press, 2004. Print.

---. *Toward the African Revolution: Political Essays*. Trans. Haakon Chevalier. New York: Grove Press, 1988. Print.

Galtung, Johan Vincent. 'Violence, Peace and Peace Research'. *Journal of Peace Research* 6.3 (1969): 167–91. Print.

Gibson, Nigel C. 'Living Fanon?'. *Living Fanon: Global Perspectives*. Ed. Nigel C. Gibson. New York: Palgrave Macmillan, 2011. 1–10. Print.

Hall, Stuart. 'Introduction: Who Needs Identity?'. *Questions of Cultural Identity*. Ed. Stuart Hall, and Paul du Gay. London: Sage, 2003. 1–17. Print.

Hegel, G. W. F. *Encyclopaedia of the Philosophical Sciences in Basic Outline Part I: Science of Logic.* Trans. and ed. Klaus Brinkmann, and Daniel O. Dahlstrom. New York: Cambridge UP, 2010. Print.

Howarth, David R. *Poststructuralism and After: Structure, Power and Agency*. New York: Palgrave MacMillan, 2013. Print.

Hudis, Peter. 'Frantz Fanon's Contribution to Hegelian Marxism'. *Critical Sociology* (2015): 1–9. Print.

Jean-Marie, Vivaldi. *Fanon: Collective Ethics and Humanism*. New York: Peter Lang, 2007. Print.

Jenkins, Richard. *Social Identity*. 2nd ed. London: Routledge, 2004. Print.

Jinadu, L. Adele. *Fanon: In Search of the African Revolution*. London: KPI, 1986. Print.

Kojève, Alexandre. *Introduction to the Reading of Hegel: Lectures on the Phenomenology of Spirit.* Trans. J. H. Nichols Jr. New York: Basic Books, 1969. Print.

Kruks, Sonia. 'Fanon, Sartre and Identity Politics'. *Fanon: A Critical Reader*. Eds. Lewis R. Gordon, T. Denean Sharpley-Whiting, and Renee T. White. Oxford: Blackwell Publishers, 1996. 122–33. Print.

Laclau, Ernesto. 'Constructing Universality'. *Contingency, Hegemony, Universality: Contemporary Dialogues on the Left*. By Judith Butler, Ernesto Laclau, and Slavoj Žižek. London: Verso, 2000. 281–307. Print.

---. 'Identity and Hegemony: The Role of Universality in the Constitution of Political Logics'. *Contingency, Hegemony, Universality: Contemporary Dialogues on the Left*. By Judith Butler, Ernesto Laclau, and Slavoj Žižek. London: Verso, 2000. 44–89. Print.

Laing, R. D., and D. G. Cooper. *Reason and Violence: A Decade of Sartre's Philosophy 1950–1960*. London: Tavistock Publications, 1964. Print.

Lazarus, Neil. 'National Consciousness and the Specificity of (Post) Colonial Intellectualism'. *Colonial Discourse/Postcolonial Theory*. Eds. Francis Barker, Peter Hulme, and Margaret Iversen. New York: Manchester UP, 1994. 197–220. Print.

Lee, Christopher J. *Frantz Fanon: Toward a Revolutionary Humanism*. Athens, OH: Ohio UP, 2015. Print.

Meszaros, Istvan. *The Work of Sartre. Volume One: Search for Freedom*. Sussex: Harvester Press, 1979. Print.

Nayar, Pramod K. *Frantz Fanon*. New York: Routledge, 2013. Print.

Onwuanibe, Richard C. *A Critique of Revolutionary Humanism: Frantz Fanon*. Missouri: Warren H. Green, 1983. Print.

Parekh, Bhikhu. *A New Politics of Identity*. New York: Palgrave-Macmillan, 2008. Print.

Parry, Benita. 'Resistance Theory/Theorising Resistance or Two Cheers for Nativism'. *Colonial Discourse/Postcolonial Theory*. Ed. Francis Barker, Peter Hulme, and Margaret Iversen. New York: Manchester UP, 1994. 172–96. Print.

Sartre, Jean-Paul. *Anti-Semite and Jew: An Exploration of the Etiology of Hate*. Trans. George J. Becker. New York: Schocken Books, 1976. Print.

---. *Existentialism and Humanism*. Trans. Philip Mairet. London: Metheun, 1948. Print.

---. Preface. *The Wretched of the Earth*. By Frantz Fanon. Trans. R. Philcox. New York: Grove Press, 2004. xliii–lxii. Print.

Sen, Amartya. *Identity and Violence: The Illusion of Destiny*. London: Allen Lane, 2006. Print.

Williams, Robert R. *Recognition: Fichte and Hegel on the Other*. Albany: State U of New York P, 1992. Print.

Žižek, Slavoj. *Violence: Six Sideways Reflections*. London: Profile Books, 2009. Print.

Chapter Three

Limits of Blackness

FANON CONTRA NEGRITUDE

A tiger does not proclaim his tigritude. He pounces.

Wole Soyinka

Fanon's commitment to universalism, transcending particular identities, set him on a collision course with leading Black writers from the French colonies. If Fanon, the uncompromising anti-colonialist, disrupted the narratives of white French liberals, Fanon, the universalist, challenged the assumptions of those who swore by Negritude.

The word *Negritude* was used for the first time by the Antillean intellectual and poet Aimé Césaire in a polemical essay against assimilation, published in the March 1935 issue of *L'Étudiant noir,* a Paris based publication Césaire co-edited along with the Senegalese Léopold Sédar Senghor and the French Guyanese Léon Damas. The word found its first poetic usage in Césaire's *Notebook of a Return to the Native Land* (*Cahier d'un retour au pays natal*) published in 1939. According to Césaire, it was in Haiti 'where Negritude rose for the first time and stated that it believed in its humanity and the funny little tail of Florida where the strangulation of a nigger is being completed, and Africa gigantically caterpillaring up to the Hispanic foot of Europe, its nakedness where death scythes widely' (*Notebook of a Return to the Native Land* 15). The Negro experience, Césaire appears to argue, is a universally similar response of Blacks to a condition of alienation, and is 'measured by the compass of suffering' (43).

Senghor had a similar perspective on Negritude as a universal human condition of the Black people. To him, Negritude was 'the sum total of black cultural values', and his preferred English equivalent of the expression was 'black personality' (Spleth 27). But for all its claims to a Black universalism, Negritude was in essence a response to the French policy of assimilation during the colonial period, championed by Francophone Black intellectuals who were responding to a specific situation created by French colonialism. Spleth rightly points out that

> [t]he phenomenon of rediscovering one's African past occurred almost exclusively among the Francophone African students and it has been theorized that the reaction came in part as a response to certain defects in French colonial policy such as the failure of the French to educate in their local languages or the erroneous assumptions of assimilation, an objective not adopted by the British. (23)

Spleth is not alone in this assessment. The Fanon scholar Nigel Gibson states as a fact that the champions of Negritude, based in Paris, had three things in common – 'the color of their skin, their language (French), and their colonial background' (62). Spleth adds that some of Negritude's fiercest critics, like Wole Soyinka or Es'kia Mphahlele, were born in former British colonies.

Negritude's general thrust was in poetry. 'Negritude adorns itself with a tragic beauty that finds expression only in poetry' (51), states Sartre in 'Black Orpheus', claiming that Black poetry is the most authentic and revolutionary poetry of that age. Besides being a negation of white values, it was also a forceful call to the white Other to recognise the Black: 'Put up with me. I won't put up with you' (Césaire, *Notebook of a Return to the Native Land* 23). Poetry was a means for the alienated Black man to affirm his presence as a historical subject, through an assertion of his identity from a suffering that the Other's perception of his skin colour has subjected him to, a way to reclaim his human essence. I am cautious of using a gendered language here – the discussions around Negritude, be it of the poets, Sartre or Fanon, almost always centre around the

Black male. Scholars have pointed out that the many studies and commentaries on Negritude, including those by Fanon, have omitted the contributions of Black women writers to the movement. The feminist scholar Tracy Denean Sharpley-Whiting argues in her *Negritude Women* that '[t]he masculinist genealogy constructed by the founding poets and shored up by literary historians, critics, and Africanist philosophers continues to elide and minimize the presence and contributions of French speaking black women to Negritude's evolution' (14). I shall, however, focus largely on the works of Césaire and Senghor as these were the poets that Fanon mostly engaged with.

NEGRITUDE'S POETRY

The Negritude of the male poets in question was a poignant memory of the Promised Land, the pristine land, the land of ancestors lost to colonialism, a beautiful Black Africa. In his poem *Black Woman,* Senghor describes Africa as a 'Naked woman, fathomless woman' and as an exotic 'Land of Promise' (506). While Africa was animalised as the 'dark continent' in the literature of the colonisers, the poets of Negritude humanised (more appropriately, *feminised*) the 'dark continent' through a positive affirmation of a Black civilisation, Black values, Black beauty and Black past. Such a view elicited severe criticism from other Black activists. The South African Es'kia Mphahlele strongly contests Senghor's eulogy of Africa: 'Who is so stupid as to deny the historical fact of Negritude as both a protest and a positive assertion of African cultural values? . . . What I do not accept is the way in which too much of the poetry by it romanticizes Africa – as a symbol of innocence, purity and artless primitiveness' (32). The Nigerian scholar Abiola Irele, to whom the themes of Negritude were a counter-movement to the cultural dependence on the West, writes in the defence of the movement:

> The quest for new values thus leads the black writer to self-definition in terms that are non-western, and the association between the black race and Africa acquires a new meaning: instead of being a source of shame, it becomes a source of

> pride. This is the ultimate end of negritude, and much of the literature is dedicated to a rehabilitation of Africa, a way of refurbishing the image of the black man. ('Negritude-Literature and Ideology' 508)

It can be further inferred from Irele's arguments that Negritude's racial exaltation of Black Africa is but a defence against the colonial apparatus that sought to socially and psychologically inferiorise the Black people, and that the use of the myth of a noble and pure Africa was 'an attempt to recreate an emotional as well as an original bond beneath the contingencies of a particularly difficult historical experience' (Irele, 'Negritude-Literature and Ideology' 511).

Negritude's poetry was essentialist – a sort of essentialism in reverse. Senghor, for instance, opines that analytical reason is European while intuitive reason is African, and at times pushes the argument to say that *reason* itself is European while *emotion* is African. According to Senghor, the European mind is essentially 'static, objective, and dichotomic. It is dualistic in that it makes an absolute distinction between body and soul, matter and spirit. It is founded on separation and opposition: on analysis and conflict. The African, on the other hand, conceives the world, beyond the diversity of its forms, as a fundamentally mobile, yet unique, reality that seeks synthesis' ('Negritude' 48).

Césaire too questions European modernity from a 'Black' perspective. The Blacks were

> those who invented neither powder nor compass
> Those who could harness neither steam nor electricity
> Those who explored neither the seas nor the sky
> But those without whom the earth would not be earth (*Notebook of a Return to the Native Land* 34)

This fundamental Black innocence was a cause for celebration:

> Eia for those who never invented anything
> for those who never explored anything
> for those who never conquered anything
> but yield, captivated, to the essence of things
> ignorant to surfaces but captivated by the motion of all things
> indifferent to conquering, but playing the games of the world. (35)

Black innocence is contrasted with the maliciousness of white colonial conquest, Black affinity to nature with white domination of culture, and a virgin Black premodernity with the penetrative and corrupting white modernity. To reject the colonial Other's discourse, the poet of Negritude uses stereotypes created by the Other to define the Self. As Césaire clarifies in an interview in 1967 to René Depestre, 'Negritude' was an act of defiance and the words *negre* and *negritude* were a violent affirmation of the self in a white world that chose to assimilate the Blacks or ignore their contributions in toto (*Discourse on Colonialism* 89).

Negritude subverted the French language to bring out as a positive affirmation those attributes of the Blacks that were given a negative image by the colonisers, attempting to negate the all-consuming white discourse of colonialism. But its excessive reliance on the discourse framed by the white Other as a reference point for the Black Self became the subject of severe criticism. Renate Zahar argues that 'this negative, revolutionary response to colonialism is deeply marked by what it rejects: it bears itself racist features. . . . The relativity of negritude stems from the fact that it has to rely on the methods of colonial ideology to react against it; even in the act of negating colonialism it reproduces its features' (67). Another criticism laid on Negritude intellectuals was that they were confining themselves to a narrow particularism.

However, in the defence of the proponents of Negritude, Irele writes, 'In their search for identity, the adherents of negritude have had to accept and explore to the full their particular situation. But, although preoccupied with a sectional and limited interest, they were inspired by a universal human need for fulfilment. In this, they have never strayed from the central, enduring problem of the human condition' ('Negritude-Literature and Ideology' 523). In order for them to embrace a universal human condition, the Blacks had to first embrace the particular situation of their racial condition.

Let us consider Césaire's passionate appeal, in detail:

> But if someone asks me what my conception of Negritude is, I answer that above all it is a concrete rather than an abstract coming to consciousness. What I have been telling you about – the atmosphere in which we lived, an atmosphere

> of assimilation in which Negro people were ashamed of themselves – has great importance. We lived in an atmosphere of rejection, and we developed an inferiority complex. I have always thought that the black man was searching for his identity. And it has seemed to me that if what we want is to establish this identity, then we must have a concrete consciousness of what we are – that is, of the first fact of our lives: that we are black; that we were black and have a history, a history that contains certain cultural elements of great value; and that Negroes were not, as you put it, born yesterday, because there have been beautiful and important black civilizations. At the time we began to write, people could write a history of world civilization without devoting a single chapter to Africa, as if Africa had made no contributions to the world. Therefore we affirmed that we were Negroes and that we were proud of it, and that we thought that Africa was not some sort of blank page in the history of humanity; in sum, we asserted that our Negro heritage was worthy of respect, and that this heritage was not relegated to the past, that its values were values that could still make an important contribution to the world. (*Discourse on Colonialism* 91–92)

Césaire's Negritude appears a 'politics of recognition' in the Taylorian sense, framed for a Black as a being-in-the-world who has been denied his due in society and in history. The Black seeks, then, not an abstract particularism but a universalism that will recognise his concrete particular condition. Hear Césaire:

> for entrenched as I am in this unique race
> you still know my tyrannical love
> you know that it is not from hatred of other races
> that I demand of myself to become a hoer for this unique race
> that what I want
> is for universal hunger
> for universal thirst (*Notebook of a Return to the Native Land* 38)

Césaire is thirsty for, is hungry for, and he *demands*, a universalism that will recognise the Black as a unique being-in-the-world. The politics, like the poetics, of Negritude is a demand for a multicultural society where 'Black' as a distinct identity – an identity born out of the shared experience of suffering – and its history, culture and values would be respected. What would this multicultural society of the future be like and what would be the role of the Black in it? In his famous tract, *Discourse on Colonialism* (1950), a work that had an immense influence on Fanon, Césaire argues that Negritude's ideal political future would be a society which was inclusively modern, where the Black, as a Black, still maintained his roots to a pristine past. Quite ironically, Césaire, who was a member of the French Communist Party till 1956, gave the Soviet Union as an example worthy of emulation. One might wonder if Césaire was referring to the rehabilitation of Russian nationalism under Stalin. Along with his celebration of 'Negro' pasts, there is a socialist undercurrent to Césaire's writings:

> Once again, I systematically defend our old Negro civilizations: they were courteous civilizations.
>
> So the real problem, you say, is to return to them. No, I repeat. We are not men for whom it is a question of "either-or." For us, the problem is not to make a utopian and sterile attempt to repeat the past, but to go beyond. It is not a dead society that we want to revive. We leave that to those who go in for exoticism. Nor is it the present colonial society that we wish to prolong, the most putrid carrion that ever rotted under the sun. It is a new society that we must create, with the help of all our brother slaves, a society rich with all the productive power of modern times, warm with all the fraternity of olden days. (*Discourse on Colonialism* 51-52)

It is probably such a sentiment in Césaire that brings Benita Parry to support him, arguing that 'Negritude is not a recovery of a pre-existent state, but a textually invented history, an identity effected through figurative operations and a tropological construction of blackness as a sign of the colonised condition and its refusal' (182). Generally, scholars have viewed Césaire's Negritude as more political, while Senghor's is perceived to be cultural. In Africana philosopher Reiland Rabaka's eyes, Senghor's culturalism was 'a comprador for racial colonial policy, racial colonial anthropology, and racial colonial ethnology' (174). Senghor's Negritude has elicited sharp responses from scholars who posit a 'good political' Negritude to the 'blank cultural' Negritude. For instance, Paulin Hountondji argues that 'for Césaire the exaltation of black cultures functions merely as a supporting argument in favor of political liberation, in Senghor it works as an alibi for evading the political problem of national liberation' (159–60). However, the point where both supporters of Césaire and Senghor reach an agreement is Sartre's view of Negritude, and Fanon's view of Sartre's view of Negritude.

ORPHIC TRAGEDY OR A 'GREAT BLACK MIRAGE'?

Sartre lent his support to the Negritude movement as it developed in the hands of Senghor, Césaire and Damas. His 'Black Orpheus', the preface to an anthology of 'Negro' poetry by West Indian and African poets compiled by Senghor and published in 1948, remains the most influential, and probably the most controversial, statement on Negritude written by a supporter.

Sartre opens his preface by saying that the Black writers in the volume are fixing their gaze on the white man, who has thus far enjoyed 'the privilege of seeing without being seen' (13). Whiteness was a claim to 'the secret white essence of things', like virtue, like truth (13). Whiteness consolidated a white universality, 'the mythic idea that White represents the very essence of existence' (Haddour 289). One of the primary functions of Negritude is to challenge this claim. The 'wild and free looks', the 'quiet and corrosive looks', of the Negritude poets 'ate away' the white claims to universalism by their contestation that the human essence was not white.

Sartre recognises the need for Negritude's particularism. 'These black men are addressing themselves to black men about black men; their poetry is neither satiric nor imprecatory: it is an awakening to consciousness' ('Black Orpheus' 16). Yet, he also tries to demonstrate that Negritude is an appeal to a universalism, even though of a different kind, one that would recognise the Black: 'I should like to show that this poetry which seems racial at first is actually a hymn by everyone for everyone' (16). Through Negritude, the Black, through a necessary consciousness of his situation as a Black being-in-the-world, eventually reclaims a humanity denied to him. The Black is a victim of the situation created by the white capitalist enterprise, not owing to his position as a class but

> *because he is a black man* and insofar as he is a colonized native or a deported African. And since he is oppressed within the confines of his race and because of it, he must first of all become conscious of his race. He must oblige those who have vainly tried throughout the centuries to reduce him to the status of a beast, to recognize that he is a man. (18; italics in original)

This observation led Sartre to coining his controversial definition of Negritude – 'anti-racist racism'. This elicited polarised responses from scholars dealing with Negritude. Mikela Lundahl claims that Sartre's misconception of Negritude was owing to an ignorance of his own identity as a privileged white male (83–96), whereas Abiola Irele completely agrees to Sartre's terminology, inferring that Sartre was only referring to a racial consciousness and not a feeling of racial superiority ('A Defence of Negritude' 9–11). Sartre writes,

> The negro cannot deny that he is negro, nor can he claim that he is part of some abstract colorless humanity: he is black. Thus he has his back up against the wall of authenticity: having been insulted and formerly enslaved, he picks up the word 'nigger' which was thrown at him like a stone, he draws himself erect and proudly proclaims himself a black man, face to face with white men. The unity which will come eventually, bringing all oppressed peoples together in the same struggle, must be preceded in the colonies by what I shall call the moment of separation or negativity: this anti-racist racism is the only road that will lead to the abolition of racial differences. ('Black Orpheus' 18)

Negritude, thus, is manifested as an 'anti-racist racism', but it is the only avenue open to the Negro for an authentic freedom and would ideally lead to the abolition of racial differences. Appropriating a Hegelian dialectic, Sartre posits white supremacy as the thesis and Negritude as the antithesis, the synthesis being a classless society without racism. Sartre perceives Negritude as a 'weak moment' in the progression of the dialectic, which leads to the transcendence of racism and ultimately to a pluralist society. Negritude is a means and cannot be an end in itself.

Hence the title to the preface to the anthology of Negritude poetry, 'Black Orpheus'. Like the tragic Greek poet Orpheus, who descends into hell to retrieve his beloved but loses her on reaching ground, the Black poet descends into his existential hell to retrieve Blackness only to lose it later once he hits the surface of humanity. 'Thus Negritude is for destroying itself, it is a "crossing to" and not an "arrival at," a means and not an end' (49).

Sartre concludes,

> It is when negritude renounces itself that it finds itself; it is when it accepts losing that it has won: the colored man – and he alone – can be asked to renounce the pride of his color. He is the one who is walking on this ridge between past particularism – which he has just climbed – and future universalism, which will be the twilight of his negritude; he is the one who looks to the end of particularism in order to find the dawn of the universal. (51)

Much like in *Anti-Semite and Jew,* Sartre opines that it is the socialist revolution in which the Black will play a positive role, and the establishment of a classless society that will put an end to racism and herald a genuine universalism. Till then, the anti-racist racism of Negritude is but a passing phase in the dialectic.

Fanon's engagement with Sartre on these contentious passages in 'Black Orpheus' has been a subject of considerable debate among Fanon scholars. In fact, it would not be an exaggeration to say that Fanon's engagement with Negritude is mediated by his dialogue with Sartre on the subject. Fanon had an uneasy relationship with Negritude. 'Sympathetic', 'empathetic', 'ambivalent', 'acerbic' and 'hostile' are all words that can be used to describe Fanon's reaction to Negritude in his works. As we shall see, it is this response to Negritude that will be an important factor in shaping Fanon's concept of identity politics that we discussed in the earlier chapter.

The very first mention of Negritude in *BSWM* is as a reaction to Sartre's categorisation of the same as a 'minor term of a dialectical progression'. Arguing that 'Black Orpheus' was an intellectualisation of Black experience, Fanon proclaims that Sartre destroyed 'black zeal' – Fanon needed, as a 'Black' himself, to lose himself completely in Negritude (103). 'Without a Negro past, without a Negro future, it was impossible for me to live my Negrohood. Not yet white, no longer wholly black, I was damned. Jean-Paul Sartre had forgotten that the Negro suffers in his body quite differently from the white man' (106). Fanon expresses his discontent with Sartre when he says,

> When I read that page, I felt that I had been robbed of my last chance. I said to my friends, "The generation of the younger black poets has just suffered a blow that can never be forgiven." Help had been sought from a friend of the colored peoples, and that friend had found no better response than to point out the relativity of what they were doing. (141)

Fanon here alludes to the uniqueness of the lived experience of the Black in a racist society, where, without the intervention of Negritude, an authentic way forward was not possible.

But then, Fanon emphatically says, 'In no way should I dedicate myself to the revival of an unjustly unrecognized Negro civilization. I will not make myself the man of any past. I do not want to exalt the past at the expense of my present and of my future' (*BSWM* 176). Fanon comes full circle to Sartre's understanding that Negritude and its exaltation of race-specific culture cannot be an end in itself. In fact, his attack on Negritude's generalisations is caustic, claiming to have no wish 'to be the victim of the *Fraud* of a black world' (179; italics in original). I thoroughly disagree with Jock McCulloch's contention that Fanon became more sympathetic to Negritude with the passing of time, ironically, as the author argues, owing to Sartre's influence (53). Azzedine Haddour makes a more convincing argument that while Fanon grappled with the issue of Blackness in all his works, it is erroneous to suggest that 'this continued critical engagement with negritude demonstrates Fanon's endorsement of its ideology' (292).

Parry also concurs that Fanon's engagement with Negritude was not unproblematic. She writes, 'Fanon's writings function at a point of tension between cultural nationalism and transnationality, without 'resolving' the contradiction and without yielding an attachment to the one or the aspiration of the other' (187). She further claims that Fanon's 'wavering empathy' with the concept became an 'ambiguous critique' in his later writings (190). However, there is little room for ambiguity in *BSWM* as regards the Negritude movement. Fanon's sarcastic remarks on Negritude's glorification of a great Black past give a different account from what Parry wants us to believe.

> Let us be clearly understood. I am convinced that it would be of the greatest interest to be able to have contact with a Negro literature or architecture of the third century before Christ. I should be very happy to know that a correspondence had flourished between some Negro philosopher and Plato. But I can absolutely not see how this fact would change anything in the lives of the eight-year-old children who labor in the cane fields of Martinique or Guadeloupe. (*BSWM* 180)

Fanon, here, reflects a sentiment from Sartre's *What is Literature?* – that to write for one's age was to want to go beyond it to the future (248). Fanon concludes *BSWM* thus: 'The body of history does not determine a single one of my actions. I am my own foundation. And it is by going beyond the historical, instrumental hypothesis that I will initiate the cycle of my freedom' (180). Nigel Gibson is quite wrong when he interprets that '[f]or Sartre, negritude represents the free existentialist choice of immediacy, but for Fanon there never was a choice' (75).

Indeed, Fanon's engagement with Sartre on Negritude has been an object of interest for several academics dealing with Fanonism. Reiland Rabaka, in his *Forms of Fanonism*, spends forty-six pages in a chapter called 'Antiracist Fanonism' to desperately prove that Sartre suffered from a racist paternalism and that Fanon was well aware of this when he criticised Sartre's Hegelian analysis of Negritude. Rabaka argues that Fanon was upset with Sartre's unwillingness 'to critically engage whiteness and white supremacy, especially amongst would-be white antiracist allies, white liberals, white workers, white Marxists, and other white leftists' (87). However, Fanon suggests no such thing in *BSWM* or in any of his works. In a similar vein, Robert Bernasconi asserts that Fanon's arguments 'against' Sartre in *BSWM* might be understood today as 'a version of standpoint theory or the epistemology of provenance', but which were developed by Fanon in his time as existential phenomenology (101). Bernasconi further claims that in Fanon's criticism of Sartre, the former 'insists that Sartre should acknowledge his limitations as a white man' (103), projecting Fanon as a proponent of the primacy of lived experience in determining politics. Both these assertions are reductionist, identitarian interpretations of Fanon that I warned of in the first chapter and refuted in the second.

Fanon's criticism of Negritude progressively intensifies from *BSWM* to *WOTE.* Taking this into account, Sonia Kruks is right in identifying that 'Fanon's objection is not that Sartre is in error in asserting that *negritude* is a transitional movement. Sartre's mistake, in fact, is to have told the truth!' (131). She further asserts that in the concluding arguments of *BSWM* Fanon draws on the most radical conception of freedom that Sartre had developed in *Being and Nothingness,* going against the essentialist rhetoric in Negritude. The problem for Fanon is that the followers of Negritude advocated a return to a cultural past while they were politically removed from the ground realities of the anti-colonial struggles that were unfolding around the world. He describes this return to a mythic past as an ahistorical movement and dubs Negritude as a 'great black mirage' in which the cultural, historical and national differences of the colonised Black people were lost. Considering the search for a 'Negro people' as a source of conflict, he explicitly states his intention to understand and destroy this source (*TAR* 18). Consider this scathing attack on Negritude in 'Racism and Culture':

> Rediscovering tradition, living it as a defense mechanism, as a symbol of purity, of salvation, the decultured individual leaves the impression that the mediation takes vengeance by substantializing itself. This falling back on archaic positions having no relation to technical development is paradoxical. The institutions thus valorized no longer correspond to the elaborate methods of action already mastered.
>
> The culture put into capsules, which has vegetated since the foreign domination, is revalorized. It is not reconceived, grasped anew, dynamized from within. It is shouted. And this headlong, unstructured, verbal revalorization conceals paradoxical attitudes. (*TAR* 42)

Fanon finds no revolutionary praxis for a genuine decolonisation in such a purely 'culturalist' approach. One could say along with the Black Marxist scholar Adele Jinadu that Fanon's quarrel with Negritude was that 'it tended to become a form of mystification, elitist in orientation and direction; above all, it lacked a populist vision; it did not constitute a radical ideological program; rather, it became an ideology of collaboration with the West' (220). We will return to this argument in the concluding chapter when we discuss the politics of the film *Black Panther* (2018).

In *WOTE*, Fanon adds to this criticism of Negritude. The argument he presents, that Negritude is not revolutionary enough, complements Sartre's views in 'Black Orpheus', though in a much stronger and direct fashion. Fanon identifies two reactions of the elites among the colonised to culture. Initially, when forced to choose between the culture of the coloniser and the native tradition, this elite goes with the former. Later, some members of the elite, during the period of decolonisation, abandon the culture of the coloniser in which they were hitherto assimilated, and seek anchorage in their native culture. To Fanon, however, the native elite's attempt to rehabilitate the native culture is nothing but 'a banal quest for the exotic' (*WOTE* 158). By the time of writing *WOTE,* Fanon had come to irrevocably dismiss Negritude along with its essentialist rhetoric as a backward looking ideology. McCulloch is right to point out that Fanon was opposed to this because '[t]his abstraction appears in the practice of lumping all Negro people under a single category, thereby denying the heterogeneity of Negro experience. Like the colonial racists, the poets of negritude presume race to be the determinant of the individual's social identity' (46). The racial politics of Blackness and anti-racist racism were not enough.

SARTRE TO BLAME?

Albert Memmi, a Tunisian writer, Fanon's contemporary and author of *The Colonizer and the Colonized,* writes that 'it was Fanon's particular tragedy that, while henceforth he hated his former colonizer, he never again returned to Negritude and the West Indies' (16). He blames this on the influence of Sartre's 'Black Orpheus' and *Anti-Semite and Jew.* Sartre's account of non-recognition as oppression, together with his forceful call for the oppressed to authentically affirm their identity, is found in *Anti-Semite and Jew.* To Sartre, it is the Anti-Semite who creates the Jew, and the situation in which the

Jew finds himself, 'an ensemble of limits and restrictions', is created by the Anti-Semite, and it is as a being-in-a-situation that the Jew makes his choices (69). The most common response from the Jew is that of 'flight', either into assimilation or into a universalist rationalism where the particularities of the Jewish condition can be avoided. Sartre dubs both as inauthentic choices. In contrast to the 'inauthentic' Jew, Sartre describes the 'authentic' as the one who demands recognition for what he is. And now follows an important passage from *Anti-Semite and Jew*, for understanding the Sartrean influence on Fanonian politics:

> If it is agreed that man may be defined as a being having freedom within the limits of a situation, then it is easy to see that the exercise of this freedom may be considered as *authentic* or *inauthentic* according to the choices made in the situation. Authenticity, it is almost needless to say, consists in having a true and lucid consciousness of the situation, in assuming the responsibilities and risks that it involves, in accepting it in pride or humiliation, sometimes in horror and hate. (90; italics in original)

Anticipating later critiques of liberal universalism, Sartre argues that the old style abstract humanism of the liberal democrat is not merely inadequate, but itself oppressive. Liberal universal humanism handicaps the Jew – not only does it seek to suppress the particularities of concrete groups, it also obscures the dynamics of oppression behind the screen of a universal human essence. While he warns against the democrat's assimilationist rhetoric which converges with that of the anti-Semite in denying the Jew his place in society, in Sartre's eyes, proper assimilation does not pertain to the liberal democrat's schema which puts difference under erasure. It does not exact from the Jew conformity and submission in the name of universalism. Rather, Sartre insists that this assimilation must be based on an ethics that respects the difference of the Jew. He thus rails against the twin danger to the 'authentic' Jew:

> For a Jew, conscious and proud of being Jewish, asserting his claim to be a member of the Jewish community without ignoring on that account the bonds which unite him to the national community, there may be not so much difference

> between the anti-Semite and the democrat. The former wishes to destroy him as a man and leave nothing in him but the Jew, the pariah, the untouchable; the latter wishes to destroy him as a Jew and leave nothing in him but the man, the abstract and universal subject of the rights of man and the rights of the citizen. (57)

Drawing from Sartre's ideas, Fanon is explicit on the question of recognition – 'He who is reluctant to recognize me opposes me' (170), he says in *BSWM*. Consequently, his starting point in *BSWM* is the problem of authenticity. To Fanon, the colonised Black people are a product of a socially produced and real situation of inferiority which they have internalised. They thus suffer from a 'psycho-existentialist complex' that prevents them from realising an authentic Self. The social origin of the Black's neurosis lies in the attitude of the white colonial society to Blackness. Appropriating Sartre's notion of the overdetermined otherness of the Jew, Fanon writes, 'I am overdetermined from the outside. I am not the slave of the "idea" that others have of me but of my appearance' (*BSWM* 87). But while the Jew can attempt assimilation through invisibility, the fact of Blackness prevents the Black from doing the same. Like Sartre's Jew, Fanon's Black too engages in flight. 'The young black in the Antilles . . . identifies himself with the explorer, the bringer of civilization, the white man who carries truth to savages—an all-white truth. There is identification—that is, the young Negro subjectively adopts a white man's attitude' (114).

Another response is to escape into the universal, much like the Jew, much more specifically for Black intellectuals who try to evade their racialised situation by an appeal to reason or other transcendental universals. The strategy of authenticity deployed by the Blacks, then, might appear to be Negritude, wherein the affirmation of Blackness, a Black culture and a Black past is seen as an end in itself. But as mentioned above, Fanon's attitude towards this is critical in *BSWM* and hostile in *WOTE*. Sonia Kruks correctly identifies Fanon's political position that 'the affirmation of identity can be liberating *only* in the context of a struggle also to transform wider material and institutional forms of oppression' (133; italics in original). Fanon's conceptualisation of identity politics, as we discussed earlier, was one shaped not by affiliations and recognitions of cultural pasts, but a call for a reciprocal recognition within the present with the intention of transcending *all* particularist identities towards a new universalist humanism.

UNDERSTANDING FANON'S INTENTIONS

One would assume that Fanon is rather explicit in his position on Negritude if only one were to read passages of Fanon as part of the whole of his works, and not as scattered isolated sentences. *BSWM* is indeed much more prone to various misinterpretations than the acidic *WOTE*, largely owing to the complex nature of the subjects addressed. Scholars – white, Black and Brown – have misinterpreted Fanon's engagement with Sartre, some arriving at ludicrous conclusions. Among other things, *BSWM* is also a work of social satire executed with ironical wit. It is worthy to cite Fanon at large here to clear any questions on his ambiguity as regards Negritude:

> Why write this book? No one has asked me for it.
>
> Especially those to whom it is directed.
>
> Well? Well, I reply quite calmly that there are too many idiots in this world. And having said it, I have the burden of proving it. (*BSWM* 1)

Who is *BSWM* directed to? Who are the 'idiots' Fanon wants to prove wrong?

> The problem is important. I propose nothing short of the liberation of the man of color from himself.
>
> We shall go very slowly, for there are two camps: the white and the black.
>
> Stubbornly we shall investigate both metaphysics and we shall find that they are often quite fluid.
>
> We shall have no mercy for the former governors, the former missionaries. To us, the man who adores the Negro is as "sick" as the man who abominates him.
>
> Conversely, the black man who wants to turn his race white is as miserable as he who preaches hatred for the whites.
>
> In the absolute, the black is no more to be loved than the Czech, and truly what is to be done is to set man free. (2)

And what does Fanon want to see done?

> Concern with the elimination of a vicious circle has been the only guide-line for my efforts.
>
> There is a fact: White men consider themselves superior to black men.
>
> There is another fact: Black men want to prove to white men, at all costs, the richness of their thought, the equal value of their intellect. (3)

The above passages should make it clear that Fanon satirised not just the fallacies of white racism and the phenomenon of Black skins wearing white masks, but, equally, the attempts of the Negritude thinkers to prove the distinctiveness of being Black – Fanon saw *Black skins wearing Black masks* as equally pathological. He did not subscribe to the idea of a rigid racial Self-love or hatred of the Other, even if it was in the service of resistance. It is not in the scope of this book to analyse the intentions behind the several scholars dealing with Fanonism who have overlooked these theoretical 'facts' and have misinterpreted Fanon. A general observation can be made though. A tendency among such scholars is to project Fanon as a messiah primarily for those who identify as 'Black'. At the risk of sounding polemical, one may state that this is as fallacious as an argument that Marx was the messiah of white workers. Provincialising Fanon is not only theoretically unproductive, it also does much injustice to the thinker. Fanon was a revolutionary humanist and a universalist, and it is those universalising tendencies in his works that alone can enable him to be appropriated in the study of identity politics at large.

We shall attempt this in a study of anti-caste politics in India in the next chapter.

REFERENCES

Bernasconi, Robert. 'The European Knows and does not Know: Fanon's Response to Sartre'. *Frantz Fanon's* Black Skin White Masks*: New Interdisciplinary Essays.* Ed. Max Silverman. New York: Manchester UP, 2005. 100–111. Print.

Césaire, Aimé. *Discourse on Colonialism.* Trans. John Pinkham. New York: Monthly Review Press, 2000. Print.

---. *Notebook of a Return to the Native Land.* Trans. Clayton Eshleman and Annette Smith. Middletown: Wesleyan UP, 2001. Print.

Fanon, Frantz. *Black Skin, White Masks.* Trans. Charles Lam Markmann. London: Pluto Press, 2008. Print.

---. *The Wretched of the Earth.* Trans. Richard Philcox. New York: Grove Press, 2004. Print.

---. *Toward the African Revolution: Political Essays.* Trans. Haakon Chevalier. New York: Grove Press, 1988. Print.

Gibson, Nigel C. *Fanon: The Postcolonial Imagination.* Cambridge: Polity, 2003. Print.

Haddour, Azzedine. 'Sartre and Fanon: On Negritude and Political Participation'. *Sartre Today: A Centenary Celebration.* Eds. Adrian van den Hoven, and Andrew Leak. New York: Berghahn Books, 2005. 286–301. Print.

Hountondji, Paulin. *African Philosophy: Myth and Reality.* Indianapolis: Indiana UP, 1996. Print.

Irele, Abiola. 'A Defence of Negritude'. *Transition* 13 (1964): 9–11. Print.

---. 'Negritude-Literature and Ideology'. *The Journal of Modern African Studies* 3.4 (1965): 499–526. Print.

Jinadu, L. Adele. *Fanon: In Search of the African Revolution.* London: KPI, 1986. Print.

Kruks, Sonia. 'Fanon, Sartre and Identity Politics'. *Fanon: A Critical Reader.* Eds. Lewis R. Gordon, T. Denean Sharpley-Whiting, and Renee T. White. Oxford: Blackwell Publishers, 1996. 122–33. Print.

Lundahl, Mikela. 'Negritude – An Anti-racist Racism? (Or Who is the Racist?)'. *Negritude.* Eds. Isabelle Constant, and Kahiudi C. Mabana. UK: Cambridge Scholars Publishing, 2009. 83–96. Print.

McCulloch, Jock. *Black Soul, White Artifact: Fanon's Clinical Psychology and Social Theory.* Cambridge: Cambridge UP, 1983. Print.

Memmi, Albert. 'The Impossible Life of Frantz Fanon'. Trans. Thomas Cassirer, and G. Michael Twomey. *The Massachusetts Review* 14.1 (1973): 9–39. Print.

Mphahlele, Es'kia. 'Negritude – A Reply'. *Critical Perspectives on Léopold Sédar Senghor.* Ed. Janice Spleth. Colorado: Three Continents Press, 1993. 31–35. Print.

Parry, Benita. 'Resistance Theory/Theorising Resistance or Two Cheers for Nativism'. *Colonial Dicourse/Postcolonial Theory*. Eds. Francis Barker, Peter Hulme, and Margaret Iversen. New York: Manchester UP, 1994. 172–96. Print.

Rabaka, Reiland. *Forms of Fanonism: Frantz Fanon's Critical Theory and the Dialectics of Decolonization.* Plymouth: Lexington Books, 2010. Print.

Sartre, Jean-Paul. *Anti-Semite and Jew: An Exploration of the Etiology of Hate.* Trans. George J. Becker. New York: Schocken Books, 1995. Print.

---. 'Black Orpheus'. Trans. John MacCombie. *The Massachusetts Review* 6.1 (1965): 13–52. Print.

---. *What is Literature?* Trans. Bernard Frechtman, Oxon: Routledge, 2010. Print.

Senghor, Léopold Sédar. 'Black Woman'. Trans. Lucille Clifton. *The Massachusetts Review* 15.3 (Summer 1974): 506–07. Print.

---. 'Negritude: A Humanism of the Twentieth Century'. *I am Because We are: Readings in Black Philosophy*. Eds. Fred Lee Hord, and Jonathan Scott Lee. Amherst: U of Massachusetts P, 1995. 45–54. Print.

Sharpley-Whiting, T. Denean. *Negritude Women*. Minneapolis: U of Minnesota P, 2003. Print.

Spleth, Janice S. *Léopold Sédar Senghor*. Boston: Twayne Publishers, 1985. Print.

Zahar, Renate. *Frantz Fanon: Colonialism and Alienation.* Delhi: Aakar, 2010. Print.

Chapter Four

Anti-Casteist Casteism?

A FANONIST STUDY OF ANTI-CASTE POLITICS

> . . . man is characterized above all by his going beyond a situation, and by what he succeeds in making of what he has been made . . .
>
> Jean-Paul Sartre

In November 2012, mobs belonging to the vanniyar caste, an intermediate caste group numerically dominant in northern Tamil Nadu, went on a rampage in Dharmapuri district and burnt down hundreds of Dalits homes and vandalised properties. The violence was instigated by inflammatory speeches made by some vanniyar community leaders who condemned an inter-caste marriage between a Dalit man and a vanniyar girl. This was followed by violence by vanniyar outfits in May 2013, where they caused significant damage to public property. Commenting on these incidents and trying to explain the cause of the anti-Dalit violence in the state, one critic lays the blame on the non-brahmin movement[1] of the previous century, arguing that the movement was 'misrepresented as an anti-caste movement, which it certainly was not', alleging that it only privileged the intermediate castes at the expense of the Dalits (Anand). On the other hand, M. S. S. Pandian, historian and Subaltern Studies scholar, argues in a commentary that the Tamil Nadu state as a whole benefitted from the non-brahmin movement and that the violence perpetrated against Dalits was more owing to the intermediate castes' desire to symbolically compensate for their loss of erstwhile authority on the upwardly mobile Dalits through such acts of violence ('Caste in Tamil Nadu – II').

Anti-Dalit violence in Tamil Nadu has been highlighted as the failure of the Dravidian movement by critics, with some attributing it to an inherent problem in the political discourse of Periyar E. V. Ramasamy (Periyar hereafter). Periyar (1879–1973), an anti-caste social thinker who challenged the socio-political domination of the brahmin castes in colonial and postcolonial India, is a household name in Tamil Nadu, and a central, but controversial, figure in Tamil politics. The key leader of the Self-Respect movement, his endurance as an icon is credited to his contributions towards the political assertion of non-brahmin castes (Geetha and Rajadurai, *Towards a Non-Brahmin Millennium*; Pandian, *Brahmin and Non-Brahmin*). While these accounts acknowledge his contributions to the Tamil non-brahmin polity, critiques that endorse the standpoint of particularist Dalit identity politics (see Gorringe, *Untouchable Citizens*) accuse him of overlooking specific concerns of the 'untouchable' castes, thereby contributing to the marginalisation of those castes. The anti-Dalit violence in recent times does give substance to the argument that a common platform, *a common identity,* for Dalits and intermediate castes was not forged in the course of the Dravidian movement. What was the problem in Periyar's political discourse that prevented a common identity or a common identification for Dalits and intermediate castes from emerging?

A Fanonist critique of Periyar's identity politics helps address this question. This intervention seeks to contribute to a critique of not just the identity politics of Periyar, but of anti-caste politics as a whole. While it would require a much larger study to discuss anti-caste movements in India as a whole, this chapter takes Periyar's anti-caste discourse as a case, building upon our previous discussions on Fanon's perspectives regarding identity politics, to evolve a framework for understanding anti-caste politics. The comparison of Periyar with Fanon is pertinent owing to the latter's perspicacious insights into the dialectic between particularity and universality in the identity politics of marginalised groups. This chapter hopes to throw light on the tensions within Periyar's discursive strategies, starting with his use of the inferiorised identity of 'shudra' as a signifier to mobilise non-brahmin intermediate castes. A Fanonist critique also helps to assess how Periyar's perception of the brahmin Other as a political enemy with a fixed identity, and of Dalits as allies whose particularities should be respected, might have contributed to the fragmentation of the political Self – in this case, the non-brahmin bloc – that his movement sought to mobilise. This can help us understand better why a political unity among intermediate castes and Dalits appears elusive.

THE 'SHUDRA' IDENTITY OF THE NON-BRAHMIN AND 'ANTI-CASTEIST CASTEISM'

A key term that Periyar used as a device for self-description and as a challenge to the brahminical ideology was 'shudra', the Sanskrit word which denotes people belonging to the lowest order in the Hindu caste system. To Periyar, the intermediate Tamil castes were shudras who were, according to his hyper-literal reading of the Hindu texts, 'sons of prostitutes of the brahmins, hereditary slaves, those who should not read, those who should not accumulate wealth' (*Kudiarasu*, 8 December 1929). The shudras were different from the untouchable Dalit castes, and Periyar, referring to this difference on several occasions, had chided the intermediate Tamil castes for their pride in their relative superiority over the Dalits.

It is here that a comparison with Negritude helps. Like the proponents of Negritude, Periyar's discourse appropriated a condescending term associated with an inferiorised identity and used it to unsettle the 'mainstream' discourse of Indian nationalism. In an article in 1938 titled 'Nationalist Milk for the Brahmin Snake', he polemically argues that the brahmins with the aid of M. K. Gandhi seized the small liberties granted by the British for themselves and duped the shudras (*Kudiarasu,* 13 March 1938). Like the Negritude thinkers who criticised the universalism of Western Enlightenment for being deeply entrenched in white superiority and racism, Periyar was opposed to Indian nationalism, accusing it of being a cover for brahmin dominance. However, unlike the Negritude thinkers, Periyar did not eulogise a pristine 'pre-contact with the Other' past or romanticise the 'noble savage' uncorrupted by modernity. To Periyar, the shudra Tamils needed to 'rise above a state of barbarism' and for that 'it is not enough that one hates god, religion, the Vedas, the traditional puranas, temples, festivals and religious processions. One also must detest the Tamil language which upholds the puranas and religious epics. This is so because the Tamil language is structured so as to degrade the Tamil' (*Periyar kalanjiyam* 138–39). He criticises the Tamil language and literature for their inherent sexism. Further, he calls on the Tamils to ignore the Tamil language and learn English, English customs and English modernity (140). According to Periyar, 'English governance, English education, English customs and English civilization have over time dented to some extent the caste system and caste hierarchies' (*Kudiarasu,* 13 March 1938). The shudra Tamil needed to give up not just the brahminical religious texts and scriptures but also her/his attachment to a native Tamil culture, to be an individual with self-respect. But whatever she/he might do, the shudra would remain a shudra as long as a brahmin remained a brahmin. That is, the symbolic presence of the brahmin rendered the intermediate Tamil castes as shudras.

Yet another difference from Negritude is that Periyar, as Geetha notes, 'did not grant epistemological privilege to experience' and was convinced that identity must be subject to 'reason, dialogue and argument' (164). This is a Fanonian sentiment at its core. Geetha further observes that to Periyar, the agent of history 'was neither the shudra, nor an adi-dravida; nor was it a Tamil or a dravida. Instead, it was the non-brahmin historic bloc, in its entirety that was to undertake the tasks of creating a new social, economic and ethical order' (163). Geetha argues elsewhere that Periyar was particular about respecting the specificities of the Dalit identity, but we will come to that shortly. While it is true that Periyar's agent of history was an abstract and fluid non-brahmin category, his discourse around caste, when addressed to the intermediate castes, addressed them as 'shudras'. He highlighted aspects of their 'shudrahood', their ritual inferiority to the brahmin castes, while also mercilessly lampooning shudra notions of superiority over Dalits, and patriarchy. He located the ideological source of the oppression of all castes in brahminism, the greatest beneficiaries being the brahmins themselves. The casteist terminology of the brahmin elite is reversed and is held up to them as proof of their complicity in the degraded social status of the rest of the population.

Ambedkar notes that 'while making themselves into a caste, the Brahmans, by virtue of this, created Non-Brahman caste; or, to express it in my own way, while closing themselves in they closed others out' (29). The brahminical ideology made the shudra in history through various religious and mythological texts, and the assertion by the brahmin of her/his identity in the present had the effect of reiterating the shudrahood of the intermediate Tamil castes. In rhetorical fashion, Periyar argues that even a brahmin of a low class would identify the intermediate castes as shudras and 'sons of prostitutes' and herself/himself as a higher brahmin identity (*Periyar kalanjiyam* 149), and Periyar asserts that the only way out would be for Tamils to secede from the Indian union (156). But he does this without supporting an alternate nationalism or national consciousness, with his sole argument as regards state power being that the Indian nation-state privileged brahmins and thus condemned the Tamils to being in the state of shudras and to untouchability. To take from Fanon, the brahmin might have made the shudra, but it is the shudra who fashions her/his politics of resistance.

We discussed in the previous chapter how and why Fanon criticised the proponents of Negritude and their 'anti-racist racism' for the limited scope of their politics. But this criticism cannot be blindly extented into a criticism of Periyar's political discourse, as his 'anti-casteist casteism', as mentioned above, did not seek legitimation in myriad pasts or through the valorisation of a pure identity. A Fanonist critique must take into consideration the nuances of Periyar's discourse and the social problem he dealt with.

Fanon was quick to observe that Negritude's privileging of an inferiorised identity, its fetishisation of the Black skin, would inevitably lead to a compromise with the system of oppression. Based on an identity shaped by the oppressor, it loses purpose without the oppressor. The shudra who accuses the brahmin of making her/him as such is already implicated in brahminical discourse.

If she/he cannot escape its grasp, she/he will try to make peace with it without authenticity and in bad faith. Periyar's usage of the shudra terminology does not divest it of its traditional negative meaning and ascribe it a positive value. Rather, he uses it to condemn those who have condemned the rest of the lower castes to a lower status. Even Periyar's non-brahmin agent of history has her/his identity based only on not being a brahmin.

To a point, the 'shudra' as an identity may strategically serve as a negative reminder to the non-brahmin castes of their need to reject and challenge brahminism. Yet, its consistent deployment by Periyar inadvertently makes the symbol of the brahmin as a permanent referent, the Other without whom the Self would collapse into vacuum. Those from the vanniyar caste who were involved in the violence against Dalits in 2012 firmly resist being called shudras – they fashion themselves as kshatriyas, the warrior caste grouping. The term 'shudra' is viewed by the vanniyars, as it is by other intermediate castes, with aversion as it is a fixed signifier that can only refer to a low social standing, a painful reminder of one's inferiority vis-à-vis the brahmin Other, a negative identity. And they would rather, within the system of social hierarchy, perpetrate violence on those lower to them than form a shudra–Dalit alliance against brahminism, which would necessitate embracing the negative connotations of their identity. Through a reading of Sartre's *Anti-Semite and Jew,* Fanon observes that '[i]n reaction against anti-Semitism, the Jew becomes an anti-Semite' (*BSWM* 141). A similar process is in operation here – to escape shudrahood, the shudra seeks a higher place in the brahminical system.

Fanon rejects a 'Negro' identity politics that is based only on the lived experiences of Blacks and their histories of suffering, in favour of a broader African politics. His endorsement of the Algerian identity is based on its affirmative potential to have an existence independent of the French. The past does not validate the politics of the present. The present has to create an affirmative politics of the future. 'I have not the right to become mired by the determinations of the past' (*BSWM* 179). Periyar's shudra, however, was determined purely by the past, or to be more specific, by a particular reading of the past. The shudra of the present was in her/his inferior social state owing to a straight succession of events from the time when the Sanskrit scriptures were composed and brahmins, generation after generation, prevented any move to achieve social equality. Periyar's equating of the Dravidian and non-brahmin intermediate castes with the shudra, and his contempt for a Tamil national identity, created the lack of an alternative affirmative identification.

The Periyarite radical was one who identified with an inferior identity and used it to deconstruct the discourse of the dominant system. But she/he was, for all practical purposes, dependent on the Other's categorisation of her/his Self as a ritual inferior. There is little or no clue of what would happen to the shudra identity in a post-brahminical scenario. Is the shudra identity, as Sartre commented on Negritude, a 'passing phase in the dialectic' or an end in itself? Is the politics of the shudra a perpetual cycle of anti-casteist casteism? In a Fanonist understanding, the implication of Periyar's political discourse is this – there is one destiny for the shudra, and it is the brahmin.

THE BRAHMIN OTHER

In 1926, the wife of the colonial governor of Madras Presidency was taken on a tour of the famous Madurai Meenakshi Amman temple by a brahmin priest. Commenting on this, Periyar, in an editorial written for *Kudiarasu* ('Republic', the party paper of the Self-Respect movement) said that while it was acceptable for a brahmin to entertain the 'coloniser', an 'alien', someone who 'shared no values with your native religion', it was unacceptable for the brahmin to allow temple entry to those belonging to the nadar caste, a low-caste group in Tamil Nadu, who were natives and technically belonged to the Hindu religion (*Kudiarasu*, 17 January 1926). He further said,

> Just as the Whites who divided us and prevented us from achieving unity and by this strategy, they ruled a country of 330 million, ruling with the aid of guns and cannons, looting our wealth, the Brahmins have divided us into several castes, instructing us that one was high and the other was low, facilitated a conflict between the high and low and with the aid of the weapons of Vedas, the scriptures, puranas, mores have

> inferiorized us and live off our blood. (*Kudiarasu*, 17 January 1926)

Though some critics from the Left claim that Periyar in his pursuit of social reform 'drifted into shameful collaboration with British imperialism' (Ram 68), he clearly understood the pernicious effects of British rule. He was also, much like Fanon, aware that the colonial system relied on native elite groups for administrative purposes. Fanon argues that in colonised underdeveloped countries, there is no genuine bourgeoisie 'but rather an acquisitive, voracious, and ambitious petty caste, dominated by a small-time racketeer mentality, content with the dividends paid out by the former colonial power' (*WOTE* 119), and was convinced that this group must be opposed by a genuine decolonisation struggle. He devotes an entire chapter in *WOTE*, 'The Trials and Tribulations National Consciousness', to discuss the malignant character of the native elites in the process of decolonisation and in the postcolony, 'since this caste has done nothing else but prolong the heritage of the colonial economy, thinking and institutions' (120).

Periyar shared a similar hostility towards native elites who spearheaded the Indian nationalist struggle and who were its representatives in Tamil Nadu. He argues that while in the initial stages, 'the poor, the peasantry, the working class' participated in the anti-colonial movement, it was only the 'brahmins who emerged as the main representatives of Tamil Nadu' (*Kudiarasu*, 03 January 1926). In his introduction to *Puratchi* (Revolution), another paper of the Self-Respect movement launched in November 1933, Periyar wrote that

> 'Puratchi' was not launched to destroy the White master and install the Black master. 'Puratchi' was not launched to end White government and bring in Black government. Nor was 'Puratchi' launched to abolish Hinduism and propagate Islam or Christianity.
>
> 'Puratchi' was born to make a revolution to end the rule of all capitalist classes and all religions, to ensure that all people live with self-respect and that there is universal equality between the male and female genders. (*Puratchi,* 26 November 1933)

This resonates with Fanon's appeal that '[i]f we really want to safeguard our countries from regression, paralysis, or collapse, we must rapidly switch from a national consciousness to a social and political consciousness' (*WOTE* 142). In the chapter on national consciousness, Fanon also discusses the role that the national party, which once was the lead advocate of decolonisation, plays in the creation of the elite. He argues that in several newly liberated African countries the national party 'operates on a tribal basis. It is a veritable ethnic group which has transformed into a party' (*WOTE* 126). In similar tones, Periyar alleges that the national party in both colonial and postcolonial India is a party that comprises entirely brahmins and their slaves (*Viduthalai*, 04 June 1968). Further, in postcolonial India, non-brahmin Tamils were enslaved through 'independence' and their oppression in multiple levels was facilitated by the domination of brahmins in the national party, arguing that brahmin domination was the consequence of Indian national unity.

There is a crucial difference between Fanon's and Periyar's approaches to the native elite. To Fanon, the 'caste' he refers to is a political and economic elite that took over the reins of colonialism, a comprador class in the postcolony. Whereas to Periyar, the brahmin caste was an inflexible sociocultural and political elite that predated colonialism, prospered during colonialism, and would dominate non-brahmins in the postcolonial condition by virtue of their ritual superiority. Fanon argues that decolonisation is essentially good, but native elites will try to wrest control and suppress the masses, and that they should be opposed for that reason; Periyar's concerns are that the native elites have oppressed the masses prior to the arrival of the coloniser, and while colonialism is essentially bad, brahminism is worse, and a temporary collaboration with the 'lesser evil' can be justified provided it creates awareness among non-brahmin castes about the nature of power relations in the country.

Periyar was reluctant to reduce his political discourse to a Manichean either/or argument, that it was either 'freedom' or 'colonialism', and he problematised what freedom meant, who it benefitted and who it excluded. Periyar's conviction was that as bad as the British rule was, independent India, under what he believed would be a brahmin rule, would be worse if there were no adequate checks and balances to curtail the dominance of the brahmin castes. In a speech in Dharmapuri district in 1967, Periyar argued that the white man was opposed because he was an alien and so too, the brahmin must be opposed since he also was an alien. He said,

> Though the White man ruled us, he gave us rights; he considered us as human beings; he ate in our homes; he wouldn't take a bath on touching us. The Brahmin is not like that. Doesn't he believe that he needs to take a bath for merely touching us? . . .
>
> We belong to this country. We do the labour that is required for the sustenance of humanity; shouldn't we question why we should continue being sons of prostitutes and Shudras to the Brahmins? Why should our women be Shudra women and prostitutes to the Brahmins? (*Viduthalai*, 11 December 1967)

Where Fanon believed that colonialism was fundamentally a dehumanisation of human beings and that it was an effort in making 'the colonised confess the inferiority of their culture' (*WOTE* 167), Periyar insisted that in the case of Tamil Nadu, the culture of the native brahmin elites had condemned a vast majority to inferiority by ritual sanction for centuries and it was colonial modernity, to some extent, that provided a space in the public sphere for the participation of erstwhile lower castes. Given this condition, to Periyar, a limited 'collaboration' with the British was justified insofar as it weakened the hegemony of the brahmin Other.

In his career in politics, Periyar was uncompromisingly opposed to brahminism. To Periyar, brahmins were interested in political power 'for their self-advancement, for the welfare of their own caste' (*Kudiarasu,* 05 November 1933). In his speeches and writings, Periyar polemically attacks the ritual inaccessibility of the brahmin Other, the privileges that the Hindu religion bestows upon them, their caste purity, their role in maintaining caste hierarchy, their role in engendering patriarchy, and their monopoly over the state apparatus. Brahminism as ideology was embodied in the agent of the brahmin, and an emancipatory politics was impossible without dislodging brahmin overrepresentation in the public sphere. Periyar's concern was that the brahmin minority, who were ordained by religion to be superior to the rest of the population, who were privileged not just by the colonial administrative and education system where they constituted the bulk of native representation, but also by the nationalist parties where they were overrepresented, would use the instruments of the postcolonial nation-state to the advantage of their own while making the rest of the populace subscribe to their ideology.

It has been discussed how 'reciprocal recognition' was central to Fanon's conception of identity politics. To Fanon, 'without reciprocal recognition there could be no identity, no self-worth, no dignity' (Bulhan 114). The Other was an enemy to the extent that the Other failed to recognise the person of colour or the colonised. But once the colonial status was done away with, there would be a mutual enriching of cultures based on a new universalism. But to Periyar, the problem begins with the moment of recognition. When the brahmin is recognised as a brahmin, it automatically implies that the non-brahmin Other who recognises him is lower to her/him. The non-brahmin is 'overdetermined from without' by the presence of the brahmin. The Jew was the slave of the idea that others had of him and the Black was the slave of his own appearance (*BSWM* 95), but the non-brahmin was the slave of the presence of the brahmin. In the case of the Jew the anti-Semite was the problem, in the case of the Black the white racist was the problem, in the case of the non-brahmin the brahmin was the problem. In Periyar's discourse, the brahmin's corporeal being and the rules and meanings that elevated him to a superior status were one and the same.

In an appreciative note, Nietzsche claims that brahmins maintained purity despite the 'dirt of politics', and that they 'felt removed and outside, a people of higher, over-kingly tasks' (54). In Tamil Nadu, with the onset of the Dravidian movement, it was this purity and the exclusiveness of the brahmin participant in the public sphere that became the focus of political criticism. It was this caste 'purity' of the brahmin castes and their ritual superiority that was, according to Periyar, responsible for the perpetuation of social hierarchy among the rest of the masses. The brahmin was not just someone whom the non-brahmin was not; the brahmin was someone whom the non-brahmin could never be. For while

Dalits and intermediate castes could move up the social ladder through the process of Sankritisation, the brahmin status was closed once and for all. The brahmin Other, by virtue of her/his caste purity, inaccessibility and fixed place in social hierarchy, was beyond reform. So in Periyar's opinion, the secular brahmin, the Indian nationalist brahmin, the communist brahmin or the Hindu nationalist brahmin were all products of, and representatives of, brahmin privilege. In the realm of the political, in a Schmittian sense, the brahmin was the Absolute Enemy. But Periyar's idea of war on the enemy was not a war of physical annihilation or any form of violence against the person. If his conceptualisation of political action to be taken against the enemy were to be summarised in a single sentence, it would be this – 'When we meet a Brahmin we must greet him "Come on you Bastard!"' (*Declaration of War on Brahminism* 16). The encounter of the non-brahmin Self with the brahmin Other was to be accompanied by a performance of ridicule at the latter, condemning her/him for inferiorising the former.

This is where the non-brahmin identity emerges at its intersubjective best. The subjectivity of the non-brahmin agent is locked in an eternal combat with the subjectivity of the brahmin agent. The brahmin – not by appearance or by idea, but by his 'pure', 'over-kingly' presence – constitutes the non-brahmin of Tamil Nadu, binding the latter as shudras and Dalits. Sartre discusses this phenomenon of the 'externally above' force creating the community of the oppressed:

> The "master," the "feudal lord," the "bourgeois," the "capitalist" all appear not only as powerful people who command but in addition and above all as *Thirds:* that is, as those who are outside the oppressed community and *for whom* this community exists. It is therefore for them and *in their freedom* that the reality of the oppressed class is going to exist. They cause it to be born by their look. (*Being and Nothingness* 442; italics in original)

I shall expand more on Sartre's argument in the next section and discuss its implications for the intermediate castes and Dalits. But here, it can be seen how in Periyar's discourse, the brahmin is the 'Third' who creates the identity of the non-brahmin condition, of that of the shudras and the Dalits. We must consider here 'the implications of recognizing that the identity of the other is constitutive of the self' (Norval 157). In a compelling observation, Laclau writes that 'as the identity of the newly emancipated groups has been constituted through the rejection of the old dominant ones, the latter continue shaping the identity of the former. The operation of inversion takes place entirely within the old *formal* system of power' (31; italics in original).

This is a plausible explanation for the fissures within the non-brahmin castes, to explain why the intermediate castes turned on Dalits once they had attained greater political power. In the case of vanniyar identity politics, the self-identification of vanniyars as kshatriyas and their violent reaction against Dalits is shaped not by a vanniyar ideology or an intermediate caste ideology, but by an implicit reference to a social hierarchy where the brahmin is permanently fixed at the apex and the vanniyars climb up by stepping on those below.

Though the original act of closure, as observed by Ambedkar, was performed by brahmins, Periyar's discourse reaffirms this closure and does little to break it. In fact, Periyar's discursive trajectory is dictated by an assumption that the brahmin identity is immutable: the brahmin who supposedly came into the region more than two millennia ago along with the 'Aryan invasions'[2], the Tamil brahmin of the present and the brahmin of the future were the same and unalterable. While Periyar was flexible and non-parochial as regards the Dravidian identity (Pandian, 'Nation Impossible' 69), the brahmin was excluded from identifying with 'Dravidianess' because of her/his fundamental inability to give up her/his 'brahminhood'.

It would be helpful here to consider Fanon's essay on 'Algeria's European Minority'. To Fanon, the minority of Europeans and European Jews who inhabit the colony were subjects who were not just products of the colonial system, but also subjects who in turn conditioned the system. He recognises the subjectivities of these privileged minorities and the choices that they make in being complicit with, neutral to, or opposed to, the system of colonialism. Fanon attaches, as an appendix, the testimony of one 'Algerian

European' who writes, 'For the Algerians I am no longer an ally. I am a brother, simply a brother, like the others' (*ADC* 176). Fanon's unconditional recognition of the European coloniser as an enemy is complemented by the conditional recognition of the European as a friend, the condition being that she/he gives up identification with the oppressor and identifies with the oppressed. The discursive strategy of this essay is that by invoking an Algerian identity that accommodates the European, it not only disturbs the notion that the Algerian nation is something primordial but it also dislocates the argument of the fixedness of the white–European identity. As Laclau argues, 'The reference to the other is also maintained here but, as the inversion takes place at the level of the universal reference and not of the concrete contents of an oppressive system, the identities of *both* oppressors and oppressed are radically changed' (31; italics in original).

Commenting on Black identity politics in America, Slavoj Žižek writes that 'it is not enough to find new terms with which to define oneself outside of the dominant white tradition – one should go a step further and deprive the whites of the monopoly on defining *their own* tradition' (*First as Tragedy, Then as Farce* 120; italics in original). Fanon does more than this when he appropriates universal humanism from the Europeans and posits it against them as a moral checkmate. He says,

> All elements for a solution to the major problems of humanity existed at one time or another in European thought. But the Europeans did not act on the missions that was designated them and which consisted of virulently pondering these elements, modifying their configurations, their being, of changing them and finally taking the problem of man to an infinitely higher plane. (*WOTE* 237)

Sartre is *both* right and wrong when he says that *WOTE* is *about* the Europeans but never *to* the Europeans (Preface xlv). *WOTE* is definitely not addressed to the European complicit in colonialism, but it does consider the European reader who acknowledges Europe's failings and engages in the project of a new humanism. By ceasing to be exclusivist like Negritude, Fanon's humanism complicates the situation – and the identity of the individual belonging to the oppressor's group. Given the universally accommodating character of Fanon's humanism, one can only be inhumane if one chooses to oppose it or even if one remains neutral. The element of choice is left open to the oppressor, and it is now the 'white man's burden' to prove his humanity as the onus is upon him.

In contrast, in Periyar's politics, the brahmin is given no choice. The obvious counterargument to this is that the brahmin gave no choice to the lower castes. The Sartrean–Fanonist rejoinder would be that such determinism was an act of *mauvaise foi,* bad faith. But one has to concede to Periyar, and to his contemporaries like Ambedkar, that they saw no ideal worthy of appropriation in brahminism or from brahmins – to do so would be to accept casteism. Fanon's frustration was that Europe had betrayed its humanism. Periyar's and Ambedkar's quite legitimate contention was that there was no humanism whatsoever in the Hindu–brahminical religion. The brahmin was not betraying an ideal he claimed to represent. He *was* that ideal and that ideal was a casteist social hierarchy. Ambedkar, who fought for adequate political representation for Dalits and constitutional safeguards for them, after several scholarly analyses of Hinduism, proposed conversion to Buddhism as a way out of the caste system. Periyar provided an extensive and uncompromising criticism of brahminism and its institutions, and suggested as a possible solution the separation of Tamil Nadu, but without effectively articulating or endorsing a self-sustaining identity and relying on the inferiorised identity of 'shudra' as a weapon for his critique.

Apart from this, a Fanonist criticism of Periyar's discourse would be its failure to unsettle the brahmin identity. By considering the brahmin as fixed for all time, the brahmin's closure of her/his identity gets validated. But leaving the brahmin the option of joining an emancipatory political project by giving up her/his identity would have placed a greater moral pressure on the 'absolute enemy' of the Self-Respect movement. And if the brahmin was fixed in her/his place, could the Dalit critic not argue that so were the intermediate castes?

THE DALIT PARTICULARITY

It was discussed above how the presence of the brahmin creates the non-brahmin identity. But the non-brahmin identity is not a homogeneous one. The identity appears self-explanatory – anyone who is not a brahmin is a non-brahmin. Technically, it is something like a 'non-vegetarian' identity. One can eat all kinds of meat, or only some types of meat, eat meat on all days, or only on some days, but all of these fall under the label of 'non-vegetarian' since they are *not* vegetarians. Similarly, a vanniyar, a Dalit, a nadar, a rajput, an Englishman, a Sunni Muslim or a German Protestant would all be non-brahmins since they are not brahmins. Periyar uses the term loosely to refer to, though not restricting it to, the intermediate castes and Dalits. These castes are given a common political platform as 'Us non-brahmins' by virtue of an external Third, the brahmin, who is beyond reach and unrealisable. Sartre writes on the Third contributing to the becoming of the 'Us':

> We are "Us" only in the eyes of Others, and it is in terms of the Others' look that we assume ourselves as "Us." But this implies that there can exist an abstract, unrealizable project of the for-itself toward an absolute totalization of itself and of *all* Others. This effort at recovering the human totality cannot take place without positing the existence of a Third, who is on principle distinct from humanity and in whose eyes humanity is wholly object. This unrealizable Third, is simply the object of the limiting-concept of otherness. (*Being and Nothingness* 442)

The brahmin, as observed above, is in the position of the Third who gives political significance to the merging of the intermediate castes and Dalits as a totality. In the politics of the Self-Respect movement, the brahmin is the external totaliser who creates the totalisation of the non-brahmin entity. Sartre writes that the concept of the Third is 'one with the idea of God' but in the absence of God 'the effort to realize humanity as *ours* is forever renewed and forever results in failure' (444; italics in original). Periyar denounced the Hindu religion and Hindu gods as creations of brahmins for the exploitation of the rest. His political discourse marked the brahmin as the secular god, the Third who can never enter the human community of the non-brahmin by virtue of his 'overman' status, a status secured by the religious doctrines created by the brahmin. But does the absence of this god result in the failure of the non-brahmin project, or does it fail owing to its own irreconcilable internal contradictions?

In an article on the politics of identity/difference in the 'Black Consciousness' ideology in South Africa, David Howarth writes that 'the signifier' "black" makes possible the creation of a black solidarity and unity, and engenders political struggle, based on a common identity actively denied by white domination. It thus functions as a nodal point unifying different subjectivities and interests against the various manifestations of white oppression' (67). The 'non-brahmin' as signifier is intended to have a similar effect in Tamil society, to create solidarity among the intermediate castes and Dalits, and to unite plural subjectivities against brahminism, *but* based on an identity that is affirmed by brahmin domination. It is here that Periyar's approach towards the question of Dalits requires critical examination.

Periyar was conscious of the unique position that the Dalit occupied in the social hierarchy. In a way, they were the reverse of everything the brahmin stood for. While brahmins could not be ritually approached by the shudra because the former were 'too clean', Dalits were to be avoided because ritually they were 'too unclean'. Just like the brahmin caste at the apex was permanently closed-off to the intermediate castes, Dalits were also closed-off to the rest. While brahminhood was a 'No Entry' zone, untouchability was generally a 'No Exit' zone.

Dalit history and the history of Dalit resistance in Tamil Nadu have their own rich narratives, and it is not in the scope of this chapter to explore that. Geetha and Rajadurai claim that, in colonial modernity, 'expression of a distinctive dalit sensibility predated the political expression of non-brahminism in the Tamil regions of the old Madras Presidency and eventually came to constitute an important and decisive flank of the non-brahmin movement' ('Dalits and Non-Brahmin Consciousness in Colonial Tamil Nadu' 2091). Several intellectuals from the Dalit castes like Iyothee Thass, Rettamalai Srinivasan and Masilamani wrote about the oppression that the untouchables faced and the unjust social structure sanctioned by brahminism. But it should be noted here that these intellectuals, who were either contemporaries of or immediate predecessors to Periyar, were also in favour of an alliance between the intermediate castes and Dalits. The movement for Dalits as a separate entity gained momentum only in the 1990s, after the supposed failure of this alliance (Gorringe, 'Taming the Dalit Panthers' 54). So what was it in the Dravidian movement that caused the failure of its emancipatory potential?

In his observations on the pitfalls in a secular political project, William Connolly notes that '[t]he historical modus vivendi of secularism, while seeking to chasten religious dogmatism, embodies unacknowledged elements of immodesty in itself. The very intensity of the struggle it wages against religious intolerance may induce blind spots with respect to itself' (4). Periyar was acutely aware of the problems within the secular project of non-brahminism, and that the non-brahmin intermediate castes had a tendency to look down upon Dalits by being relatively superior in a society structured like a pyramid. Contrary to the accusations of those who claim that he was insensitive to Dalit particularities, Periyar was in fact very keen to address the issue, and in several cases, he sided with Dalits over the intermediate castes. For instance, in the 1957 Mudukulathur riots between the thevars, a numerically dominant intermediate caste in southern Tamil Nadu, and Dalits, he sided firmly with the latter and called for the arrest of thevar leaders who were instigating caste violence.

Periyar does not provide the non-brahmin identity as an easy suturing of the identities of intermediate castes and Dalits. Throughout his political discourse, he is consistent when referring to the non-brahmin whole as 'us non-brahmins' or 'Dravidians' or 'Tamils' – but when addressing specific cases of intermediate castes and Dalits, he uses 'us shudras' and 'you Dalits'. This might appear problematic. Geetha and Rajadurai explain in Periyar's defence:

> Periyar was conscious of and sensitive to the specificities of dalit oppression and also of the crucial fact that the assumption of a distinctive identity by the SCs could secure much needed material succour. Besides he recognised the rights of dalits to define their political and social selves on their own terms and

> did not attempt to co-opt their emergent subjectivity into an undifferentiated and simplistic non-brahmin solidarity. At all times, Periyar was aware that this solidarity was not given but had to be constructed. ('Neo-Brahminism' 133)

While it would indeed be intellectual dishonesty to accuse Periyar of being a patron of the intermediate castes and of displaying insensitivity to Dalit particularities, the defence of Periyar's support to Dalit specificity needs to be problematised. Dalit particularism is based purely on the social construct that a specific caste is 'untouchable'. A Dalit particularist political project bases itself on the lived experience of untouchability, and its Other is everyone else in the brahminical social order who is not an untouchable. To draw from Fanonism, not only must a Dalit be an untouchable, she/he must be an untouchable in relation to everyone else. Relativity is not far from solipsism and, thus, Dalit intellectuals and activists in the state (only from the 90s) either began particularist movements that started with promise but soon fizzled out, or wrote odes to pristine pre-civilisational pasts much like the Negritude poets. The project of Dalit unity also seems quite elusive. Of the three major Dalit castes in Tamil Nadu, the pallars no longer want the Dalit label and identify themselves as a land-owning upwardly mobile caste; the paraiyars are politically militant but their political formations are largely isolationist; and the arunthathiyars, the lowest among the Dalit castes, have legitimate grievances that their concerns are suppressed by the other powerful Dalit castes (Bathran). In this scenario, a purely particularist Dalit movement would be counterproductive as it would only accentuate fissures between Dalits and other lower castes and also within themselves, preventing the emergence of a genuine, universalist struggle.

A NEW PERIYARISM, PERHAPS . . .

Periyar's discursive strategy as regards caste politics works like this: (1) the brahmin, who is permanently fixed, needs to be ridiculed; (2) the shudra, who is in thrall of brahminism, must be enlightened; (3) and the Dalit, who is oppressed by the rest, should have her/his particularity respected. An interplay of identity, difference and relativism can be observed here. Mouffe argues that it is possible to understand how identity-based antagonisms arise '[w]hen we accept that every identity is relational and that the condition of existence of every identity is the affirmation of a difference, the determination of an "other" that is going to play the role of a "constitutive outside"' (2).

The Other who unites 'Us' is never a given but is constructed in a discourse. As much as recognising the brahmin as an Other is part of Periyar's discourse, so is the recognition of the particularism of the Dalit identity. The latter opens up the possibility for a Dalit particularist to construct the intermediate castes as the Other who unites 'Us Dalits'. Indeed, some Dalit intellectuals from Tamil Nadu have alleged, through their readings of history, that just as the Aryans invaded India to oppress the Dravidians, the forerunners of the contemporary Dravidians also collaborated with the invaders to oppress the original natives of the land, Dalits (Pandian, *Brahmin and Non-Brahmin* 238–40). The flaw in Periyar's discursive strategy is not obliviousness to Dalit specificity, as his critics allege. Rather, it is the lack of an affirmative Master identity, a universal towards which the shudras, Dalits and those among the brahmins who are willing to give up their privileged status, can move. Periyar's 'incredulity towards metanarratives' and his respect for particulars open up spaces for discursive antagonisms from within the groups for whom he was fighting for.

It is true that the rioting vanniyar mob in Dharmapuri does not have an ideology of its own and is only following the cultural logic of brahminism. It is true that the intellectuals interpreting such incidents of conflict between intermediate castes and Dalits, claiming that Periyar's Self-Respect movement was intentionally in favour of empowerment of intermediate castes at the cost of Dalits, are acting in a *fetishist disavowal*, refusing to recognise the systemic nature of caste violence, that is, 'not only direct physical violence, but also the more subtle forms of coercion that sustain relations of domination and exploitation' (Žižek, *Violence* 8).

But it is also true that Periyar's discourse does not create a common identity, an affirmative identity that would enable the intermediate castes and Dalits to identify in something beyond their immediate particularities. Fanon was aware that if a white were to be criticised only for the reason that she/he was white, then that discursive strategy also provided excuses for a Black to criticise an Arab, a Muslim to criticise a Christian, purely on the basis of identity and notions, real or imagined, of the relatively privileged Other. Basing a politics on a history of oppression by the Other *alone* cannot produce a transformative praxis to create a more accommodating future and a post-casteist society. The Other – all Others – must be unsettled by a universalism that is cognisant of particulars but still opens up spaces for transcending them. Reading Periyar with Fanon may assist in that project.

NOTES

[1] The non-brahmin/Dravidian movement had its intellectual origins in the mid-nineteenth century but emerged as a mass movement from the early twentieth century, largely under Periyar's leadership. This chapter uses non-brahmin/Dravidian movement to refer specifically to the phase of the Self-Respect movement that Periyar spearheaded from the 1920s till his demise in 1973.

[2] The 'Aryan invasion theory' of lighter-skinned Aryan tribes 'invading' and subjugating the darker-skinned natives of India was floated by several Orientalist scholars. This was taken up by ideologues of the non-brahmin movement as evidence of the existence of a pre-Aryan Dravidian civilisation in south India which was later corrupted by Aryan brahmins.

REFERENCES

Ambedkar, B. R. *Castes in India: Their Mechanism, Genesis and Development*. Jalandhar: Patrika Publications, 1985. Print.

Anand, S. 'No Pink Chaddis for PMK'. *The Hindu* 13 July 2013. Print.

Bathran, Ravichandran. 'The Many Omissions of a Concept: Discrimination amongst Scheduled Castes'. *Economic and Political Weekly* 51.47 (2016): 30–34. Print.

Bulhan, Hussein Abdilahi. *Frantz Fanon and the Psychology of Oppression*. New York: Plenum Press, 1985. Print.

Connolly, William E. *Why I am Not a Secularist*. London: U of Minnesota P, 1999. Print.

Fanon, Frantz. *A Dying Colonialism*. Trans. Haakon Chevalier. New York: Grove Press, 1965. Print.

---. *Black Skin, White Masks*. Trans. Richard Philcox. New York: Grove Press, 2008. Print.

---. *The Wretched of the Earth*. Trans. Richard Philcox. New York: Grove Press, 2004. Print.

Geetha, V. 'Who Is the Third That Walks behind You? Dalit Critique of Modernity'. *Economic and Political Weekly* 36.2 (2001): 163–64. Print.

Geetha, V., and S. V. Rajadurai. 'Dalits and Non-Brahmin Consciousness in Colonial Tamil Nadu'. *Economic and Political Weekly* 28.3/9 (1993): 2091–98. Print.

---. 'Neo-Brahminism: An Intentional Fallacy?' *Economic and Political Weekly* 28.3/4 (1993): 129–36. Print.

---. *Towards a Non-Brahmin Millennium: From Iyothee Thass to Periyar*. Kolkata: Samya, 1999. Print.

Gorringe, Hugo. 'Taming the Dalit Panthers: Dalit Politics in Tamil Nadu'. *Journal of South Asian Development* 2.1 (2007): 51–73. Print.

---. *Untouchable Citizens: Dalit Movements and Democratization in Tamil Nadu*. London: Sage Publications, 2005. Print.

Howarth, David. 'Complexities of Identity/Difference: Black Consciousness ideology in South Africa'. *Journal of Political Ideologies* 2.1 (1997): 51–78. Print.

Kruks, Sonia. 'Fanon, Sartre and Identity Politics'. *Fanon: A Critical Reader.* Eds. Lewis R. Gordon, T. Denean Sharpley-Whiting, and Renee T. White. Oxford: Blackwell Publishers, 1996. 122–33. Print.

Laclau, Ernesto. *Emancipation(s)*. London: Verso, 2007. Print.

Mouffe, Chantal. *The Return of the Political*. London: Verso, 1993. Print.

Nietzsche, Friedrich. *Beyond Good and Evil: Prelude to a Philosophy of the Future*. Trans. Judith Norman. Eds. Rolf-Peter Horstmann, and Judith Norman. Cambridge: Cambridge UP, 2007. Print.

Norval, Aletta. 'Letter to Ernesto'. *New Reflections on the Revolution of our Time*. Ed. Ernesto Laclau. London: Verso, 1990. 135–58. Print.

Pandian, M. S. S. *Brahmin and Non-Brahmin: Genealogies of the Tamil Political Present.* Ranikhet: Permanent Black, 2007. Print.

---. 'Caste in Tamil Nadu – II: Slipping Hegemony of Intermediate Castes'. *Economic and Political Weekly* XLVIII.4 (2013): 13–15. Print.

---. 'Nation Impossible'. *Economic and Political Weekly* 44.10 (2009): 65–69. Print.

Ram, N. 'Pre-history and History of the DMK: *The Politics of Cultural Nationalism in South India* by Marguerite Ross Barnett'. *Social Scientist* 6.5 (1977): 59–91. Print.

Ramasamy, E. V. *Declaration of War on Brahminism*. Trans. A. S. Venu. Chennai: Dravidar Kazhagam Publication, 1998. Print.

---. *Periyar kalanjiyam: Jaathi-theendaamai, paagam 11* [Periyar repository: Caste-untouchability, part 11]. Chennai: Periyar Suyamariyathai Prachaara Niruvanam, 2011. Print.

---. *Kudiarasu* 3 January 1926. Print.

---. *Kudiarasu* 17 January 1926. Print.

---. *Kudiarasu* 8 December 1929. Print.

---. *Kudiarasu* 5 November 1933. Print.

---. *Kudiarasu* 13 March 1938. Print.

---. *Puratchi* 26 November 1933. Print.

---. *Viduthalai* 4 June 1968. Print.

---. *Viduthalai* 11 December 1967. Print.

Sartre, Jean-Paul. *Being and Nothingness: An Essay on Phenomenological Ontology*. Trans. Hazel E. Barnes. Oxon: Routledge, 2003. Print.

---. Preface. *The Wretched of the Earth*. By Frantz Fanon. Trans. Richard Philcox. New York: Grove Press, 2004. xliii–lxii. Print.

Žižek, Slavoj. *First as Tragedy, Then as Farce*. London: Verso, 2009. Print.

---. *Violence: Six Sideways Reflections*. London: Profile Books, 2009. Print.

Chapter Five

Expansive Identity and the Ethics of Resistance

THE POETICS OF THE KURDISH MOVEMENT

In order for the universe of revolutionary values to arise, a subjective movement must create them in revolt and hope.

Simone de Beauvoir

For outsiders unfamiliar to the dynamics of the Middle East, the Kurdish question can be overwhelming. Prior to their resistance to ISIS aggression, many in this part of South Asia had heard little about the Kurds. The cultural and political suppression of the Kurds in Turkey, Syria and Iran, even the genocide of the Iraqi Kurds, was rarely talked about. Also, it was not surprising to find sections of the Left assuming that the Kurds were a secessionist movement funded by Western powers with the aim of destabilising supposedly 'anti-imperialist' countries in the Middle East. There were a few who saw the Kurdish movement as a legitimate nationalist movement for a separate nation state of Kurdistan, much in the lines of the demand for a free Tamil Eelam or Catalonia. Such sympathisers often did not differentiate between the politics of the Kurdistan Democratic Party (KDP) based in northern Iraq and that of the Kurdistan Worker's Party (PKK) and its affiliates.

For a while, I was under the impression that the PKK was a progressive nationalist organisation, learning about their movement only through news articles and other secondary sources. However, in the course of a solidarity meeting organised in London by the Campaign Against the Criminalisation of Communities in 2012, I became acquainted with a prominent Kurdish activist named Mehmet Aksoy who suggested that I read the primary works of the PKK leader and Kurdish ideologue Abdullah Öcalan, for a better perspective on the movement. Aksoy and I had the opportunity to interact at other similar events, even as I learnt more about the nuances of the Kurdish struggle. Our interaction was unfortunately cut short, as Aksoy was killed in an ISIS attack in September 2017, while he was filming the operations of the YPG (Yekîneyên Parastina Gel – People's Defence Units) in Raqqa, Syria. This chapter is a small tribute to Aksoy.

In this chapter, I discuss the contemporary Kurdish movement largely through the works of Öcalan – and by 'Kurdish movement' I am referring to the PKK and its sister groups. Bringing them into a dialogue with Fanonist ideas of identity and resistance discussed in previous chapters, I introduce and expand upon the idea of 'expansive identity' and why it is imperative for an ethical resistance movement. The political vision of the PKK and its affiliates is not founded on any particular racial, ethnic, regional or religious belief, but rather on an idea, or a set of ideas, that aims to resonate with people everywhere. Kurdish fighters in Turkey, Syria and Iran claim to fight for the freedom of everyone in the region – Kurds, Turks, Arabs, Assyrians, Yazidis, Armenians and others. The formation of self-defence groups and decentralised command are integral to their project. Likewise, women's autonomy is promoted not only as an ideal but is implemented in practice. With the exception of the Tamil Tigers till 2009, no other insurgent group in history had such a significant number of women in military high command. Öcalan promotes *Jineology* (Kurdish: *jineolojî*) as a science of women's liberation and for understanding and challenging oppression in society. Fully recognising the sociocultural diversity of the region and also the differences within the Kurdish people as such, the movement does not consider the Kurdish identity to be a monolith and does not aspire for ethno-national homogeneity; the PKK instead proposes a more democratic concept of identity.

THE POLITICS OF THE PKK

It is beyond the scope of this chapter to discuss in detail the history of oppression of the Kurds and their resistance. Much like the case of the lower castes in India, discussed in the previous chapter, the Kurds have faced oppression and discrimination under several regimes in the pre-colonial, colonial and postcolonial eras. After the partition of the Middle East into nation states, the Kurds were dispersed as minorities across territories of Turkey, Iran, Syria and Iraq. 'Kurdistan' broadly refers to the geographical region inhabited by the Kurds, cutting across the borders of these countries. Turkey (from the secular military juntas to the neo-Ottomanist regime of Erdoğan), the Ba'athist regime of the Assads in Syria, and the Islamist regimes in Iran forced assimilation upon the Kurds and any resistance was met with state repression – for instance, the Iraqi Kurds endured genocide under Saddam Hussein. Opportunistically used by world powers and ditched to suffer in the hands of local despots, the popular saying that 'the Kurds have no friends but the mountains' appeared as a self-evident truth in the previous century, as many of them took to guerilla warfare to defend their homeland and their identity.

Of the Kurdish groups that emerged, the PKK was undoubtedly the most important, not only because of the central role it plays in the Kurdish movement today, but also because of its radically different approach to the idea of self-determination. The PKK was formed in 1978 as a Marxist-Leninist group which initially subscribed to the idea of national self-determination – that is, the right of nations to secede and form a nation-state of their own. Under the leadership of Abdullah Öcalan, they launched an armed insurgency in 1984 and the state repression that followed led to the loss of over 40000 lives, destruction of over 4000 villages and displacement of tens of thousands of civilians. Öcalan, who emerged as the key intellectual and theorist of the Kurdish movement, was ultimately arrested in February 1999 in Kenya by Turkish forces with the help of Western powers. Confined to solitary imprisonment ever since, Öcalan has written extensively on the Kurdish struggle, proposing solutions for a peaceful and just resolution of the Kurdish question, simultaneously suggesting alternatives to the modern nation-state model. Despite an official peace process that was initiated in 2009, arrests, intimidation and even murders of Kurdish activists continue in Turkey. Dozens of Kurdish civilians were killed in an air strike in Roboski in 2011, and three prominent Kurdish women activists were assassinated in Paris in January 2013 which many blame on the Turkish intelligence. The emergence of the People's Democratic Party (HDP) as a powerful challenger in electoral politics, promoting a 'radical democratic political project' against Erdoğan's 'right-wing conservative populism' (Tekdemir, Web, n. p.), led to further repression. Turkey's pressure and geopolitical considerations compelled several Western governments to criminalise the PKK as a terrorist organisation.

While low-intensity warfare has been carried out against the PKK and its supporters over the years and despite several human rights violations committed by the Turkish state, the Kurdish question was rarely covered in the mainstream media. It required brutal spectacles of violence by the ISIS in the Syrian crisis and their humbling defeats at the hands of the PKK-affiliated YPG for the Kurds to get some attention – women guerillas of the YPJ (Yekîneyên Parastina Jin – Women's Defence Units) made headlines for their bravery and initiative in their armed resistance to the Islamists. However, while there was much focus on what the Kurds were fighting against, there was little discussion on what they were fighting for, and the politics that informed them.

Very broadly, the Kurdish movement is socialist. Though they were initially inspired by the Soviet Union, they eventually underscored the limitations of the Soviet model.

> The main critique of the Soviet Revolution by the PKK is based on the view that it is the victim of vulgar materialism since it exhausted all the energy of socialism for the growth of the economy, party and state. The Soviet experience of socialism and its counterparts in other parts of the world were seen by the organization as a kind of "primitive" or "childish" socialism, whereas "the socialism of Kurdistan is a great human revolution which by all means does not recognize borders". According to the PKK, the state should have been dissolved in the people, but in experienced socialism the process has

> occurred the other way round; people have been dissolved in the state and party (Ozcan 102).

It is interesting to note that the PKK viewed the Soviet Union positively in the period when it understood the right to self-determination as a right to secession. The emergence of the critique of state socialism occurs simultaneously with the critique of the nation-state as an ideal. Öcalan opposes the dictatorship of the proletariat as it would ultimately result in 'a red-painted adaptation of well-known capitalist states as long as the state, as a tool, operating on the basis of force and power, is not overcome', further arguing that scientific socialism must foreground freedom and equality, and reject all forms of centralised state (*Prison Writings: The PKK and the Kurdish Question in the 21st Century* 52). He asserts quite unambiguously, 'My personal quest is for the development of an ideological system that opposes not only capitalism, but all state-based class societies' (57). To Öcalan, twentieth-century socialism failed because of its reluctance to address a key issue – 'What is a free man, what circumstances bring about a free people?' (70)

Öcalan places freedom as a higher virtue than equality. One should be careful not to reduce this to a liberal argument; rather, it comes from a radical libertarian idea that a free society might not be an equal society, but an unfree society will never be an equal society. In other words, freedom is the ultimate guarantee for equality and social justice. In a very loose sense, the politics of the PKK may be called anarcho-socialist, though Öcalan is critical of certain types of Western anarchism for their excessive emphasis on individualism. The Kurdish movement lays much emphasis on direct democracy and grassroots participation. It is of note here that Öcalan was influenced by the ideas of the American anarchist Murray Bookchin. The latter's idea of 'libertarian municipalism', the creation of local-level democratic bodies as opposed to a centralised state apparatus, contributed to the development of Öcalan's idea of 'democratic confederalism' which forms the theoretical basis for the praxis of the PKK. Jongerden argues that 'democratic autonomy and confederalism are the cornerstones of a new political discourse, defined as a meta-language that instructs its members and followers how to live and act beyond the nation-state' (246).

Öcalan outlines five key principles of democratic confederalism (*Democratic Confederalism* 33–34):

1. It is a 'contrasting paradigm of the oppressed people' to the existing nation-state model, as the formation of a new state does not guarantee the freedom of a people.
2. It is the 'cultural organizational blueprint of a democratic nation'.
3. It is based on 'grass-roots participation' and 'decision-making processes lie with the communities'.
4. It is a democracy from below that can truly accommodate the diversity of the Middle East, rejecting the solutions proposed by world powers.
5. Finally, it is an 'anti-nationalist movement', for though it aims 'at realizing the right of self-defence of the peoples by the advancement of democracy in all parts of Kurdistan' it does not intend to create a Kurdish nation-state and instead aims to create federal structures in the regions where the Kurds inhabit.

Disagreeing with orthodox Leninism, Öcalan rejects the idea of a single revolutionary party and its cadres alone being the vanguard of the people, and stresses the importance of NGOs and civil society institutions in a democratic polity (*Prison Writings: The PKK and the Kurdish Question in the 21st Century* 63), and argues that social organisations must be directly involved in decision-making processes so as to democratise power, to make it horizontal (52). Ecology and feminism are considered as important as Kurdish self-determination – in fact the very idea of self-determination itself is seen as incomplete without addressing these questions.

It is important to note that Öcalan's work is not a rejection of modernity, but a response to the crisis of modernity. In his preface to the third volume of Öcalan's *Prison Writings,* world-systems theorist Immanuel Wallerstein argues that there are two possible outcomes in the future – a non-capitalist system that retains the worst features of capitalism and a system that is relatively more democratic and egalitarian (*Prison Writings III* 12). The Kurdish movement aims to be a struggle towards the latter option. Though Öcalan sees the PKK as 'the synthesis of East and West' (*Prison Writings: The PKK and the Kurdish Question in the 21st Century* 53) he is sceptical about the European nation-state. While arguing that the Middle East should not seek to prove some essential validity of ancient civilisations, he also says that they should not blindly imitate Europe (111). One can see a Fanonian sentiment here: 'let us not pay tribute to Europe by creating states, institutions, and societies that draw their inspiration from it' (*WOTE* 239). It is worthy to consider a passage from Öcalan's *Prison Writings III* at length to get a picture of the socio-economic and ethico-political ideal of the PKK:

> The economic-social model of the democratic nation solution is the communal unit. Ecological, social, and economic social units do not aim to make profit; determining and servicing fundamental needs is essential. The market may still exist, but monopoly over it is to be restricted and placed under the ethical control of society. The ethical and political values of society are to be placed above law. Instead of the rule of law, priority is given to the principles of an ethical and political society. Criteria of direct democracy apply in the resolution of social affairs and problems, and direct democracy is proportional to the era's scientific consciousness. Freedom of society and the individual exists only when scientific consciousness, arts, ethics, and politics are intertwined. The level of freedom of the individual is linked to the level of freedom of the communal units he/she participates in. Detachment from society cannot mean freedom. (90)

In as much as it defends the rights of the individual, a democratic nation must give importance to groups, as the idea of an abstract citizen is 'liberal babbling' (*Prison Writings III* 22). The individual citizen makes sense only as a part of a community and civil society and thus, both individual and collective freedoms have to be protected. Öcalan opposes statist theories with 'democratic solution theory' which seeks to solve problems from the units of the society rather than the state, and he lays stress on social initiatives rather than statist interventions (22). Dirik aptly summarises this praxis when she says, 'the current paradigm is centered on organizing the community's direct self-determination with the communes as the most fundamental unit and method of democracy. . . . The commune in Kurdistan is therefore the proactive choice of the consciously and ethically acting, political society to reject the capitalist nation-state and actively defend itself against it' (227). We should however not make the error of mistaking democratic confederalism as a celebration of premodern localism. Jongerden addresses this arguing that 'the idea of allocating decision-making powers to local councils does not come with an inwardly oriented or parochial form of militant particularism. On the contrary, the concept of confederalism evokes a sense of connectedness, of village, neighborhood, city, and regional councils' (255). The particular is not dislocated from the universal; *the particular embodies the universal.*

One can have a Fanonian appreciation of these ideas. We saw in the previous chapters how Fanon, while unconditionally supporting anti-colonial movements, was sceptical of nationalism and was apprehensive about the future of postcolonial nation-states. Fanon argues that the national bourgeoisie of newly formed nation-states in the colonies 'mimics the Western bourgeoisie in its negative and decadent aspects without having accomplished the initial phases of exploration and invention that are the assets of this Western bourgeoisie' (*WOTE* 101). The formation of this class in the liberated colony is not organic and soon, the single party, the national leader, and an empty anti-colonial nationalist rhetoric end up serving the interests of this class. The urban elite and the landowners ensure that the development that happens favour their sectarian interests and under an incompetent bourgeoisie in an underdeveloped country, anti-colonialism quickly gives way to racism and chauvinism (103). The inter-tribal sectarian hatreds in Rwanda and Nigeria, and the Islamic, Hindu and Buddhist fundamentalisms in Pakistan, India and Sri Lanka respectively, are but a few examples where the Western Other is replaced by a local Other, with terrifying consequences. Riots, pogroms, ethnic cleansing, and even genocide, are sanctioned as these Third World countries consolidate themselves as nation-states, seeking to impose mono-religious, mono-lingual or mono-ethnic orders.

Fanon believed that to counter such political disasters in underdeveloped countries, 'the combined efforts of the masses, regimented by a party, and of keenly conscious individuals, armed with revolutionary principles, should bar the way to this useless and harmful bourgeoisie' (*WOTE* 119). He believed that such a party must have an organic relationship with the masses, and not an elitist vanguard that believes itself to be above them. It should serve a mutually pedagogic purpose. 'The party is not an instrument in the hands of the government. Very much to the contrary, the party is an instrument in the hands of the people' (127). Over the party, Fanon prioritises the community and encourages local initiatives as the only check to despotism from the top. As a critique of the one-party nation-state, he says, 'Nobody has a monopoly on truth, neither the leader nor the militant. The search for truth in local situations is the responsibility of the community' (139).

After a careful reading of Fanon, one can confidently assume that Fanon would have endorsed, in principle, the efforts of the PKK to address the Kurdish question. It is to read Fanon in such fashion, to address the problems that the contemporary world faces, as I suggested in my first chapter, that Fanonism must be seen as something more than a simple theory of anti-colonialism. A reductive reading can bring out Fanon as a defender of Arab chauvinism or Islamism in the Middle East simply because they appear to be 'anti-imperialist'. Reading Fanon's critique of identity helps us understand the ambitious identity project of the Kurdish movement better.

EXPANSIVE IDENTITY AS INTEGRAL TO A DEMOCRATIC NATION

The democratic nation, the idea espoused by Öcalan, values open cultural identities, and individual and collective freedoms (*Prison Writings III* 28). In a political climate of oppressive chauvinistic nation states where 'the Kurdish people simultaneously exist and do not exist', and '[t]he Kurds are human beings and yet they are not' (*Prison Writings: The PKK and the Kurdish Question in the 21st Century* 126), the reclamation of Kurdish identity is reclamation of their humanity. Yet, this identity project does not mean a return to the past, but is oriented towards the future. Dismissing the idea of a 'forever valid, forever immutable' Kurdish reality with the understanding that '[s]ocieties evolve dialectically within a broader framework of time and geography' (17), Öcalan urges the

Kurds to transform the past into 'a new, dialectic-driven, creative process' (29). The Kurdish movement, by overcoming 'all forms of nationalism and reactionary family and tribal structures', could play a major role in democratising the Middle East (89). The democratic nation thus formed

> is not bound by rigid political boundaries, one language, culture, religion and interpretation of history, signifies plurality and communities as well as free and equal citizens existing together and in solidarity. The democratic nation allows the people to become a nation themselves, without resting on power and state, becoming a nation through much needed politicisation. It aims to prove that not only through politicisation but also, in the absence of becoming a state or acquiring power, a nation can be created with autonomous institutions in the social, diplomatic, and cultural spheres as well as in economy, law and self-defence, and thus build itself as a democratic nation. (*Democratic Nation* 23)

While the idea of a democratic nation is grounded in the Kurdish struggle, 'It is a definition open to universality' (24). The idea of an exclusive Kurdish ancestral homeland, that only ethnic Kurds have a unique claim to, is rejected. The Kurdish homeland that the Kurdish movement envisages is not only one where Kurdish communities enjoy autonomous rights, but a place where other communities will have equal participation in the building of a political society based on secular civic values. Hence, the Kurdish movement not only attracts militant supporters from Arabs, Yezidis, Turkmen, Assyrians and other groups in the region but also leftists from Western countries leaving their homes to fight alongside the YPG and YPJ.

Fanon hoped for (in retrospect, one could say vainly) the realisation of a society founded on universal values and pluralism, in Algeria. He strongly believed that '[i]f we really want to safeguard our countries from regression, paralysis or collapse, we must rapidly switch from a national consciousness to a social and political consciousness' (*WOTE* 142). Unlike the Arab nationalists in the FLN, Fanon did not want a return to an Algeria 'identical to the situation of a century ago' but rather 'a modern Nation that can take an honourable place in the world today', which necessitates 'the destruction of colonial structures and a break with precolonial structures' (*AF* 570). Fanon believed in a 'democratic revolution' in Algeria where 'modern societal structures' would replace 'medieval and feudal structures', and he calls for both 'liberation from foreign yolk [sic] and the destruction of feudal relics from the middle ages' (570). He looked at democracy in two ways – as a cultural value that guarantees freedoms and rights for the people; as a political power that locates sovereignty in the people (572). One can see the realisation of these hopes in Kurdistan.

In the first volume of his *Prison Writings* – subtitled *The Roots of Civilisation* – Öcalan genealogically traces the crisis of modernity, beginning from the origins of civilisation in the Tigris and the Euphrates to the consolidation of the modern capitalist nation-state. He asserts, 'It is our foremost duty to bring about the birth of a new ideological identity in our minds and souls, an identity coherent and holistic, original and robust, an identity that will prevail' (247). I would like to call this *expansive identity*.

Usually in identity politics, a 'single axis of identity' takes priority (Heyes 9). It considers itself as natural and actively seeks to delegitimise challenges from within as a threat to its fight against the enemy on the outside. For instance, the Iranian human rights activist Maryam Namazie, a trenchant critic of Islamism, regularly faces censorship at public events in Britain from Muslim groups and their allies under the charge that her ideas would contribute to the climate of anti-Muslim prejudice. This sort of approach to identity takes certain identities as granted and any interrogations of such identities are censored. Wendy Brown rightly argues that '[i]n its emergence as a protest against marginalization and subordination, politicized identity thus becomes attached to its own exclusion' (74). The accusation of exclusion becomes an excuse for an exclusive identity, triggering cycles of particularist confrontations whose highest goal is tolerance of difference without a commonness of struggle. This was Fanon's charge against Negritude.

Expansive identity, on the other hand, recognises the value that identity and identification has, but does not fetishise it. While it provides its members a sense of community, it does not retain its idea of the Other based on racial, national or religious prejudices. The Fanonian plea for subjects to exercise their agency to transcend their particularisms and work towards universal solidarity is appealing here.

All politics is a *politics of identification*, of the Self and the Other. There can be no politics without identification. 'We know who we are only when we know who we are not and often only when we know whom we are against', the American conservative Samuel Huntington remarked (21). It is crucial to note that the external Other forges who 'we are' but not who 'I am'. A Hegelian would understand the resolution of the dialectic as a stage where the 'We' becomes a part of the 'I' and 'I' becomes part of the 'We'. 'We', in a political sense, has meaning only with the arrival of 'They', or the Other. Again, the Other as a political entity makes sense only when the Self is perceived as a part of a collective against the collective of the Other. In the political realm, the Other is always a terrible, threatening force who threatens to injure the political interests of the Self that identifies with a collective. In a Schmittian understanding, the individual has no political enemies, but the group cannot survive without a political enemy.

The conflict for universalism, the conflict against universalism, and conflict of universalisms, emerge at the stage where the Other is identified as the political enemy. Racist politics is always a conflict against universalism, as it involves a fundamental rejection of the universality of the human condition. A similar argument can be made for caste conflicts and politics that celebrate particularist identities, like that of Negritude. And we can see the conflict between neo-liberal regimes and pan-Islamist groups, each seeking to impose their vision on the world, as an example of the conflict of universalisms. What is important to note is that the manner in which the Other is constructed determines the nature of the politics being espoused.

A truly transformative praxis must unsettle the identity of both the Self and the Other so as to create a new paradigm of discourse where there can be a reconciliation of interests of the actors involved. It does not fetishise identity nor does it ask for a complete abandonment – it *transfigurates*. Let us say the Other is a Turk. Does the politics of the Kurdish movement allow her to transcend her identity and be a part of a common struggle? The politics of the PKK does. This is vital to assess if a politics is emancipatory or not. If the politics ossifies the Other in an essentialised identity, it cannot avoid ossifying itself into an essentialised identity, 'deeply invested in its own impotence' (Brown 70).

Nonetheless, an abstract universalism is not possible in routine politics. To speak of a 'human identity' makes as much sense to politics as to speak of 'God's children' – unless the human identity is mobilised to fight an inhuman Other or God's children are mobilised to fight godless children. Given that the understanding of the enemy in the political is still anthropocentric, such a universal can be more harmful than good, and likely to cause as much, if not more, harm than the extremist nationalist ideologies of the previous century. All universalisms must evolve or adapt to particular contexts. Likewise, all particularisms have a potential for transcendence into a universal – like Fanon's faith that both the Black person and the white person could give up their respective identities. But should there be an emphasis on transcendence in the first place? According to Connolly, a noble response in a plural society would be 'to seek to transmute cultural antagonisms between transcendence and immanence into debates marked by agonistic respect between the partisans, with each set acknowledging that its highest and most entrenched faith is legitimately contestable by the others' (47).

A noble desire indeed. But this assumes that the Others too hold the same values of agonistic respect that one professes to uphold. What if the Others are insistent that their values, their cultural practices and their objects of faith are not contestable? Worse still, what if the Others are willing to use violence to counter such legitimate contestations? Western liberal multiculturalism has no answers to these questions. One can invoke Strauss's concern here: 'whether Tolerance can remain tolerant when confronted with unqualified intolerance' (28). It is dark humour that for all their ire against Samuel Huntington's 'clash of civilizations' theses, in fact, it is precisely this multicultural liberal-left who are the true Huntingtonians of the modern times. Why? More than the right-wingers, it is they who believe that there is something called a

'Muslim world' with uniform 'Muslim sentiments', as different from the other worlds, whose inhabitants prioritise the Islamic identity over all else, and that it is a liberal duty to respect this identity. A critical interrogation of the ideology that structures this identity, or who it privileges, is to be avoided because it would invite accusations of Islamophobia. Here lies the fix of multiculturalist identity politics: in its reluctance to adopt universalism owing to fears of being assimilative, it embraces a logic similar to that of the racist, that the Other's identity is immutable, only that the multiculturalist believes that this identity must be tolerated, or even welcomed. 'To us, the man who adores the Negro is as "sick" as the man who abominates him' (Fanon, *BSWM* 2).

The reason why Fanon was suspicious of the particularist Black identity politics of Negritude of his time was not only because of its glorification of myriad pasts, but also because he believed that the simple binary mapping of Black and white obfuscated more than it revealed, often silencing other critical, more radical, voices from the colonised. Is this not what is happening now in the mainstream debates around Islamophobia? One can observe a monopolisation of the discourse on Islam by Islamists and liberal Muslims, which is being actively or passively assisted by the Western multicultural liberal-left, at the cost of those within the so-called 'Muslim world' like the Kurds who really do not place religious identity as their political priority and are instead working towards a radical political struggle and social reform within their communities. As Melinda Cooper rightly argues, 'The kind of state multiculturalism promoted by the parliamentary Left and Right has in practice tended to corroborate the most vocal claims to cultural representativeness, repeatedly privileging the Hindu and Islamic Right as the authentic voices of cultural difference to the detriment of other, dissident tendencies on the "Asian" left' (31).

There are no particular or universal identities. There are only particularist and universalist approaches to identification with identities. For instance, in a particularist approach, an anti-racist movement can target the X race as the Other and consider an inferiorised Y identity as the rallying point of a political project. However, if it is purely particularist, such a political project can only lead to *ressentiment* where Y accuses X for being superior while insisting on the exclusiveness of being Y. A critical universalist approach based on understanding identity as expansive would, while targeting the X identity for its claims to superiority, nevertheless grant members of the X community possibilities of transcending their identification with that particular identity to something different in a common political project with Y, as equal partners.

Concerning the tension between universalism and particularism, Zerilli argues, 'it is a matter not of choosing one over the other but of articulating, in a scrupulously political sense, the relation between the two' (4). A purely particularist approach to identification will take the Other's identity as complete in itself. (He is Arab, she is Black, they are Dalits, and must be respected/hated for what they are.) Whereas, a critical universalist approach considers identification with an identity as metastable, 'never purely stable, nor simply plastic' (Nancy 11), as something incomplete, with the possibility of becoming 'for-others'.

Expansive identity involves a constitutive pluralism, to take from Chantal Mouffe (19), but also a conditional pluralism. Expansive identity is constitutive of difference, but conditional on political positions. It respects the diversity of the constituent groups, but challenges prejudiced politics that members of such groups may have. Such an approach seeks neither the celebration of difference nor the erasure of difference, but involves the possibility of the transfiguration of particularist differences into something *truly different*. The Kurdish movement is not only changing the way the Kurds look at themselves; if it succeeds, it may result in radically altering the way the Turks, the Jews, the Iranians, the Arabs, and the other people of the Middle East look at their identities and their ideas of nation and nationalism.

JIN, JIYAN, AZADI

'Women, Life, Freedom' – this is a popular slogan of the Kurdish movement and captures the essence of their political priorities: gender justice, ecology and community, and freedom in the most comprehensive sense. To Öcalan, one does not take priority over the other. The Kurdish movement does not use a broad narrative to downplay the importance of the women's question. He refers to women as 'the oldest colonised people who have never become a nation' (*Liberating Life* 35) and that '[l]iberating life is impossible without a radical woman's revolution which would change man's mentality and life' (51). Thus, the PKK has a remarkably high representation of women as both cadres and leaders. Likewise, all-women units like the YPJ exercise autonomy and conduct social, political and military activities by their own initiative. Dirik argues, 'Rather than considering women's liberation as a side effect of a perceived general liberation, the Kurdish freedom movement turned it into its core principle or its "line", as democracy's guarantor and very method' (227). Dirik also notes that the concept of *Jineology* is being developed day by day as a living practice of women's liberation in the Kurdish areas in Northern Syria. In the words of a Kurdish guerrilla, 'women opened the road towards a remarkable qualitative change and transformation process in Kurdish society, as they began to constitute an organized force in the PKK. They questioned and challenged the notions of property and domination that the Kurdish man had long asserted on women' (Stêrk, Web, n. p.). Combating male dominance within their own communities is considered as important as resisting external invasion of Kurdish lands.

One should consider here Fanon's relative blindness to women's question, which has been critiqued by feminists (Mercer; Young). In Fanon, where woman is not an object of desire either for the coloniser or the colonised male, she is someone's wife, daughter or sister, who finds mention only because of her importance to the anti-colonial struggle. In 'Algeria Unveiled', Fanon defends a traditional cultural device like the Islamic veil with the argument that it served as a symbolic as well as a practical resistance to colonialism. His perspective on promotion of French liberal values for women in Algeria was wholly negative, as he considered it an integral part of the colonial strategy to separate the Algerian woman from the Algerian man, and making both feel ashamed of their national culture. This argument is not without its merits. 'Convening the woman, winning her over to the foreign values, wrenching her free from her status, was at the same time achieving a real power over the man and attaining a practical, effective means of destructuring Algerian culture' (*ADC* 39). The colonial sought to unveil the Algerian woman and the authentic act of resistance against this was for the woman to be veiled. Though he asserts, 'The Algerian woman is at the heart of the combat. Arrested, tortured, raped, shot down, she testifies to the violence of the occupier and to his inhumanity. As a nurse, a liaison agent, a fighter, she bears witness to the depth and the density of the struggle' (66), it is only the woman as an instrument of the anti-colonial resistance struggle that is of interest to Fanon. The woman who confronts the internal oppressor, the home-grown patriarch, is completely absent. Fanon underrated the role of native religion and culture and the FLN's political priorities, and believed that the Algerian woman would voluntarily unveil herself in the process of decolonisation, emerging as a free subject participating in nation building. He could have heeded the words of Simone de Beauvoir who unconditionally supported Algerian decolonisation but presciently noted that the question of Algerian women would be suppressed post-independence.

This, of course, should not be seen as a judgment on Fanon from the vantage point of a contemporary progressive movement but rather as a critique of the gaps in Fanonism so as to arrive at a more democratic approach to identity and resistance. This is important at a time when a false dichotomy is played out between the 'free Western woman' and the 'oppressed Muslim woman', especially with regard to the choice of dress and sexual lifestyles. While a section of liberals make stereotypical judgments on both, it is not uncommon to find supporters of identitarianism defending conservative Islamic values, at times invoking Fanon. The achievements of Kurdish women might enable us to step out of these binaries and read Fanon in a more sensible manner.

The Kurdish movement challenges conventional notions of nation, state and identity. If the Kurdish movement fails, the Middle East would be doomed to another century of dictatorial regimes, ethnic sectarianism and religious fundamentalism. If it succeeds, it will be an alternative to not only capitalist nation-states but also to the statist model of socialism of the previous century. Democratic confederalism and the politics of expansive identity have universal significance. They can be the prelude to the new humanism that Fanon talked about in the conclusion of *The Wretched of the Earth.*

REFERENCES

Brown, Wendy. *States of Injury: Power and Freedom in Late Modernity.* Princeton: Princeton UP, 1995. Print.

Connolly, William E. *Pluralism.* London: Duke UP, 2005. Print.

Cooper, Melinda. 'Part 1: Why I Am Not a Postsecularist'. *boundary 2* (2013) 40(1): 21–39. Print.

Dirik, Dilar. 'The Revolution of Smiling Women: Stateless Democracy and Power in Rojava'. *Routledge Handbook of Postcolonial Politics.* Eds. Olivia U. Rutazibwa, and Robbie Shilliam. Oxon: Routledge, 2018. 222–38. Print.

Fanon, Frantz. *A Dying Colonialism.* Trans. Haakon Chevalier. New York: Grove Press, 1965. Print.

---. *Alienation and Freedom.* Eds. Jean Khalfa, and Robert J. C. Young. Trans. Steven Corcoran. London: Bloomsbury, 2018. Print.

---. *Black Skin, White Masks.* Trans. Charles Lam Markmann. London: Pluto Press, 2008. Print.

---. *The Wretched of the Earth.* Trans. Richard Philcox. New York: Grove Press, 2004. Print.

Heyes, Cressida J. *Identity Politics.* New Delhi: Critical Quest, 2015. Print.

Huntington, Samuel P. *The Clash of Civilizations and the Remaking of World Order.* New York: Simon and Schuster, 2003. Print.

Jongerden, Joost. 'The Kurdistan Workers Party (PKK): Radical Democracy and the Right to Self-Determination beyond the Nation State'. *The Kurdish Question Revisited.* Eds. Gareth Stansfield, and Mohammed Shareef. London: Hurst, 2017. 245–53. Print.

Mercer, Kobena. 'Decolonisation and Disappointment: Reading Fanon's Sexual Politics'. *The Fact of Blackness: Frantz Fanon and Visual Representation.* Ed. Alan Read. London: Institute of Contemporary Arts, 1996. 114–31. Print.

Mouffe, Chantal. *The Democratic Paradox.* London, New York: Verso, 2000. Print.

Nancy, Jean-Luc. *Identity: Fragments, Frankness.* New York: Fordham UP, 2015. Print.

Öcalan, Abdullah. *Democratic Confederalism.* Trans. International Initiative. Cologne: Transmedia, 2011. Print.

---. *Democratic Nation.* Trans. International Initiative. Cologne: Transmedia, 2016. Print.

---. *Liberating Life: Woman's Revolution*. Trans. International Initiative. Cologne: Transmedia, 2013. Print.

---. *Prison Writings: The PKK and the Kurdish Question in the 21st Century.* Trans. Klaus Happel. London: Transmedia, 2011. Print.

---. *Prison Writings: The Roots of Civilisation.* Trans. Klaus Happel. London: Pluto Press, 2006. Print.

---. *Prison Writings III: The Road Map to Negotiations.* Trans. Havin Guneser. Cologne: Transmedia, 2012. Print.

Ozcan, Ali Kemal. *Turkey's Kurds: A Theoretical Analysis of the PKK and Abdullah Öcalan.* Oxon: Routledge. 2006. Print.

Strauss, Leo. *Liberalism, Ancient and Modern.* Chicago: U of Chicago P, 1968. Print.

Stêrk, Zilar. 'The Feminization of Kurdish Politics: A Guerrilla's Sociological Analysis'. *Komun-Academy.* 16 November 2018. Web. 03 December 2018. <https://komun-academy.com/2018/11/16/the-feminization-of-kurdish-politics-a-guerrillas-sociological-analysis/>.

Tekdemir, Omer. 'Left-wing Populism Within Horizontal and Vertical Politics: The Case of Kurdish-led Radical Democracy in Agonistic Pluralism'. *Journal of Balkan and Near Eastern Studies*. 2018. Web. 24 March 2019. <10.1080/19448953.2018.1497756>.

Wallerstein, Immanuel. 'Preface to the Road Map'. *Prison Writings III: The Road Map to Negotiations.* By Abdullah Öcalan. Cologne: International Initiative, 2012. 10–13. Print.

Young, Lola. 'Missing Persons: Fantasising Black Women in *Black Skin, White Masks*'. *The Fact of Blackness: Frantz Fanon and Visual Representation.* Ed. Alan Read. London: Institute of Contemporary Arts, 1996. 86–101. Print.

Zerilli, Linda M. G. 'This Universalism which is Not One'. *Diacritics* 28.2 (1998): 3–20. Print.

Conclusion

FANON AS A CRITIC OF MULTICULTURALISM

> It has never been more difficult to read Fanon than it is today.
>
> Achille Mbembe

A very popular genre among online pornography is interracial porn. Often, 'interracial' is synonymous with the coupling of a Black man and a white woman. Other combinations, like that of white men and Black women, or white men and Arab women, or Black men and Indian women exist, but they are nowhere in such high demand as that of Black men and white women. Many highly visited pornography portals cater to this. One of the racist fantasies that structure this interracial combination on porn sites is the idea of white purity being corrupted by a near-bestial Black sexuality. The standard trope in these videos is a submissive white woman being taken by a dominant hyper-masculine Black male. The sexual objectification of white woman as the ultimate object of desire occurs simultaneously with the dehumanisation of the Black man, reducing him to his penis. The caricatured Black body serves the purpose of white sexual transgression, and the focus remains firmly on the extraordinary power and abilities of the Black penis; in other words, 'one is no longer aware of the Negro but only of a penis; the Negro is eclipsed. He is turned into a penis. He *is* a penis' (Fanon 131).

While one may say that the view of Black men as hypersexual beings is not unique to modern white racism – the much earlier Arabic *One Thousand and One Nights* begins with the frame story of a Persian king's wife cheating on him with Black slaves and being brutally killed for it – it was white colonialist racism which gave a 'scientific' twist to it through a *belief* that low intelligence and hyper sexuality was an essential racial feature of the Black population (the actual fact of the average penis size of the African and the European being more or less the same was irrelevant). If there is one crucial lesson that psychoanalytic theory teaches us it is that fantasies can often influence reality more than reality influences reality – in Lacanese, the reality of desire is more terrifying than actual external reality (Žižek, *The Sublime Object of Ideology* 45). In the white racist fantasy, 'The Negro is taken as a terrifying penis' (Fanon 136), and since the racist also views himself as infinitely virile there is 'a phenomenon of diminution in relation to the Negro, who is viewed as a penis symbol' (123). Lynchings of Black men by racists in the US were often accompanied by castration where '[t]he penis, the symbol of manhood, is annihilated, which is to say that it is denied' (125). Anti-Semitic hatred towards the Jew is in the realm of the idea. The Jew is simultaneously responsible for capitalism and communism, for being invested in their identity and for being rootless cosmopolitans. With the Black, the hatred/prejudice is physical. What Fanon discovered through a survey of over 500 whites was that the image of the 'Negro' was associated with 'biology, penis, strong, athletic, potent, boxer, Joe Louis, Jesse Owens, Senegalese troops, savage, animal, devil, sin' (128).

Fanon argues in *BSWM* that the Black man is envied or hated for possessing some mystical sexual quality that the white person attributes to him. That is, the Black man possesses something that the white man lacks, which the racist simultaneously loathes and desires. According to Žižek, the Other's access to some specific form of enjoyment is a key component of racism (*The Sublime Object of Ideology* 187). It is worthwhile to do a brief Fanonist reading of how this plays out in popular cinema. If racist fantasies played out in interracial porn present the 'extra-large' penis as a special attribute of Black men, Ryan Coogler's *Black Panther* (2018) substitutes it with 'vibranium'.

Coogler's extremely successful film is the story of a power struggle in an imaginary African kingdom, Wakanda. Though outsiders think of Wakanda as an economically backward country, it is actually highly technologically advanced, powered by the strongest metal on earth, vibranium. Vibranium, which is as fictional as Wakanda, is a secret exclusive to Wakandans which few outsiders know of. Wakanda is governed by a hereditary monarchy and only those of royal bloodline can challenge or replace a reigning monarch. T'Challa (Chadwick Boseman) takes over as king after his father T'Chaka's demise. He is challenged and is temporarily overthrown by his cousin Eric Killmonger (Michael Jordan), the son of a Wakandan Black radical in the US who intended to supply weapons to the oppressed but was killed by T'Chaka. Killmonger inherits his father's radicalism and seeks to overthrow the traditional structures in Wakanda and supply vibranium to the oppressed around the world to enable them to displace the world powers. In the climax, T'Challa kills Killmonger and begins a policy of social outreach, while still remaining in the good books of America. The irony of Wakandan politics, if one follows the Marvel cinematic universe, is that vibranium is willingly shared with the likes of Iron Man and Captain America, characters who are emblematic of the worst forms of American gung-ho militarism, but not with oppressed nations of the world seeking to forge a new world order. Vibranium substitutes the penis as a fictional object of fantasy that provokes/satisfies white desire.

The commercial success of *Black Panther* was refreshing in a film industry which was used to portraying Africa as a dark continent of civil wars or savage beasts which required white intervention. Yet, the idea that governs it is quite dangerous. Wakanda's core philosophy can be described as Negritude combined with capitalist modernity – a society which retains ethnic pride and all the clannishness and hierarchies of feudal societies while reaping benefits of technology, which demands respect and cooperation from world powers but not a redistribution of resources to ailing countries. Though presented as a Black Utopia, the closest real-life equivalent to Wakanda is Saudi Arabia. Almost universally cheered by multiculturalists, *Black Panther* represents everything that Fanon abhorred in the politics of Negritude and Black particularism. The villain, Killmonger, stands closer to the Fanonian ideal – in fact, to the ideal of the real Black Panthers Party. The most revealing compliment *Black Panther* received though was from the American right-wing website *Breitbart*. A columnist wrote that 'T'Challa is big on border security, believes Wakanda and Wakandans should come first, and fiercely protects his country's culture from outsiders, including refugees. If this is all starting to sound familiar, it should' (Nolte, Web, n. p.); because to this columnist, T'Challa was like Trump and Killmonger was Black Lives Matter.

One can observe that there is a general market for exoticised identities. Other successful films in the Marvel franchise like Matthew Vaughn's *X-Men: First Class* (2011) capitalise on the question of identity, where mutants are to be read as a euphemism for the marginalised. Yet, while these films stress the importance of recognition and respect, redistribution or a radical re-structuring of society is seen as too violent. *X-Men* shows Charles Xavier (James McAvoy), a rich mutant, laying the foundation for a mutant-only school to provide a sanctuary to his kind. He recognises the hatred and fear which humans have the 'mutantkind', but believes that the goal to strive for would be a diverse society where mutants and humans live in harmony. On the other hand, Magneto (Michael Fassbender), a Holocaust survivor, distrusts humanity and believes that mutants should build a capacity to defend themselves, violently if necessary. He prevents Russian and American nuclear submarines from killing a group of mutants and in retaliation attempts to blow them up. This, however, is prevented by Xavier to whom such violence is excessive. It is important to note here that Magneto is not harming civilians but the military force of two world powers, hoping thereby to upset the balance. Xavier wants to retain the balance but work for greater accommodation within the system. In sum, this is the politics of liberal multiculturalism where acceptance of diversity and token representation replaces revolutionary upheavals. The idea that radical change is needed to upset the status quo is not a Utopian thought in these times; on the contrary, 'the true utopia is the notion that we can somehow survive with small cosmetic changes' (Žižek, *Trouble in Paradise* 32).

This is also why we must view with much scepticism the endorsement given by a section of the liberal-left to outbursts of isolated violence in some American cities in the wake of the Black Lives Matter movement. Commenting on the violence in Ferguson, Žižek, invoking Walter Benjamin's 'Critique of Violence', correctly observes that such outbursts 'with no concrete programmatic demands' are sustained 'by just a vague call for justice' ('Divine Violence in Ferguson', Web, n. p.). Indeed, Benjamin's thesis is that '[w]here mythical violence is lawmaking, divine violence is law-destroying' (25). But this is only a part of it. Benjamin further adds, 'where the first sets bounds, the second wreaks boundless destruction; where mythical violence apportions blame and calls for expiation simultaneously, divine violence expiates; where the former threatens, the latter strikes; where one is bloody, the other, albeit lethal, kills without bloodshed' (25). Did the reactive violence by the oppressed in Ferguson achieve, or even aim at, any of this? Sadly, no. The 'irrational outbursts' such as Ferguson are not symptoms of a new world order – they are symptoms of the disease of the old world order.

The advocacy of indiscriminate violence to combat white racist power centres is nothing new. In the past, Black activists like Eldridge Cleaver advocated rape of white women as a form of resistance to white racism – he later expressed regret for propagating such ideas. Life came full circle when he eventually joined the Republican Party and became a Christian conservative. What does this say? The reality is that the American system is more than capable of defending itself against such violent excesses by its minorities. If anything, it would prefer pampering such particularist minority identity politics because the postmodern logic of global capitalism requires proliferations of multiple minority identities. This impotent violence of particularist identity politics, fuelled only by anti-white *ressentiment*, creates more boundaries and comes nowhere closer to destroying them, which alone would be the real act of divine violence. So the white racists who are wont to criminalise the entire Black population and the white multiculturalists who, to overcome a misplaced sense of guilt, celebrate any and all forms Black resistance are actually conforming to the logic of the same system.

It was discussed earlier how Fanon saw as pathological both those who adored and those who hated the Black person. His message is crucial – the practice of attributing an immutable identity to an exotic Other and preaching a phobia against it, as the racists are wont to do, or preaching a patronising tolerance for it, as multiculturalists are wont to do, damages the possibility of a universalist political project. In fact, more than the Black nationalists in America, it was Martin Luther King Jr. who took this message to heart, when he argued that it was necessary to overcome Black separatism and fight on a universalist plank for all the oppressed in the country.

Of course, we must, without any hesitation, acknowledge that the police system in several parts of America is racist. But at the same time, we should not slip into the quite problematic multiculturalist position of endorsing everything that goes by the name of Black/minority identity politics. One can acknowledge that a section of the population has been systematically marginalised, convey solidarity with their struggles, while also remaining critical of reactionary cultural and political tendencies within those minority communities. We can learn a few lessons here from Lenin who, while being extremely sensitive to the precarious position of the Jews in Russia, was also boldly critical of isolationist Jewish Bundist politics. To make an excuse that reactionary identity politics of minority communities have to be tolerated just because 'they are different from us' is after all another form of racism.

In his book *Mistaken Identity,* Asad Haider defines identity politics as 'the neutralization of movements against racial oppression. It is the ideology that emerged to appropriate this emancipatory legacy in service of the advancement of political and economic elites' (n. p.). Haider, who draws much inspiration from the Black revolutionary tradition in the US, further argues that '[i]n its contemporary ideological form, rather than its initial form as a theorization of a revolutionary political practice, identity politics is an individualist method. It is based on the individual's demand for recognition, and it takes that individual's identity as its starting point' (n. p.). Promotion of diverse individuals and their experiences of culture and identity takes priority over redistribution of resources – which is why a film like *Black Panther* could be so successful while the radical aspects of the Black Panthers Party have largely faded. In the spirit of the Haitian revolutionary Toussaint L'Ouverture, Haider calls instead for an 'insurgent universality, which says that we are not passive victims but active agents of a politics that demands freedom for everyone' (n. p.).

This book is an attempt to defend the idea of such an insurgent universality. Through our discussions of Fanon's revolutionary humanism and his criticism of Negritude, we saw the limits of particularist identity politics and the need to be grounded in a universalist perspective. Framing a Fanonist critique of anti-caste politics in India, we talked about the need to unsettle the identities of both the oppressor and the oppressed. Finally, exploring the idea of expansive identity in the context of the Kurdish movement, we discussed why a universalist perspective guided by a pluralism that was constitutive of difference but conditional on political orientation could provide a democratic alternative to existing paradigms.

Reading Fanon today is pointless if the only end is to criticise racism and the relics of colonial pasts; one should read Fanon to equally criticise contemporary multiculturalist identity politics. Multiculturalism, the political belief that identities must be respected for what they are, is the language that even racists speak today. White racist demagogues like Richard Spencer decry universal values and call for preservation of the white identity which is unique and to be respected, just as Islamists claim the same for the Muslim identity. Fanonism, on the other hand, teaches that no identity is valid by itself. The body of work that Fanon produced might not come with timeless answers, but it constantly compels us to question that which is taken as fixed, and to move beyond. A politics of accusation, resentment and glorifying one's own marginality will not pose a credible challenge to the current world order. It is only a common struggle accompanied by a transcendence of narrow ethnic or religious affiliations that can contribute to an expansive concept of identity and resistance.

REFERENCES

Benjamin, Walter. *One-way Street and Other Writings.* Trans. J. A. Underwood. London: Penguin, 2009. Print.

Fanon, Frantz. *Black Skin, White Masks.* Trans. Charles Lam Markmann. London: Pluto Press, 2008. Print.

Haider, Asad. *Mistaken Identity: Race and Class in the Age of Trump.* London, New York: Verso, 2018. EPUB file.

Nolte, John. '"Black Panther" Review: The Movie's Hero is Trump, the Villain is Black Lives Matter'. *Breitbart.* 16 February 2018. Web. 11 November 2018. <https://www.breitbart.com/entertainment/2018/02/16/black-panther-review-great-actors-make-failure-launch/>.

Žižek, Slavoj. 'Divine Violence in Ferguson'. *The European Magazine.* 09 March 2015. Web. 11 November 2018. <https://www.theeuropean-magazine.com/slavoj-zizek/9774-slavoj-zizek-on-ferguson-and-violence>.

---. *The Sublime Object of Ideology*. New Delhi: Navayana, 2010. Print.

---. *Trouble in Paradise: From the End of History to the End of Capitalism*. London: Allen Lane, 2014. Print.

Glossary of Select Terms

Anti-colonialism: A vague and often abused term now, in Fanon's reading it referred to the struggle of native populations to overthrow the European colonial system in their countries.

Authenticity: Identity politics looks at 'authenticity' as a fixed certificate of belonging to a certain community. In Fanon's existentialist reading, it refers to a commitment to values one has chosen for oneself rather than being a passive recipient of values from outside.

Decolonisation: This refers to not just the mere physical and political ejection of the coloniser, but also a destruction or radical alteration of the institutions, culture and values that sustained the colonial system.

Double Consciousness: This concept was originally introduced by W. E. B. Du Bois to describe the phenomenon of Black people in America evaluating themselves by the 'standards' set by the white Other. Fanon elaborates on it to describe how the Black person either seeks to imitate the white Other or withdraws into some archaic past to construct a Black authenticity.

Existentialism: A philosophical movement that began in Europe, more specifically France, during the Second World War, which laid great emphasis on freedom, responsibility and human agency, and rejected any form of determinism. Though only Jean-Paul Sartre and Simone de Beauvoir explicitly claimed to be existentialists, other prominent thinkers like Søren Kierkegaard, Friedrich Nietzsche, Karl Jaspers and Albert Camus have also been credited for contributing to this philosophy. Fanon was strongly influenced by Sartre's reading of existentialism.

Humanism: Yet another vague term, 'humanism', very simply explained, is a philosophical project that places the human being at the centre of its interrogation, as different from a study of structures. Popularly confused with pacifism, humanism as seen by radicals is not averse to endorsing violence in the pursuit of human emancipation.

Lactification: The phenomenon of Blacks attempting to whiten their skin, through miscegenation or even discursively.

Lumpenproletariat: In Marxist terms, an unemployable section of the population who are prone to criminal and illegal activities. Fanon saw them as a highly revolutionary class in the colonies.

Negritude: A literary movement begun by Black poets from Francophone countries, it laid great emphasis on the antiquity and uniqueness of Black civilisation and identity.

Postcolonialism: An academic discipline that studies the political, sociocultural and intellectual effects of colonialism on former colonies. While Fanon's thoughts have been universally acknowledged as being important to this discipline, the question of whether Fanon was a postcolonialist or not is a matter of debate among academics.

Further Reading

Caute, David. *Frantz Fanon.* New York: Viking Press, 1970. Print.

Cherki, Alice. *Frantz Fanon: A Portrait.* Trans. Nadia Benabid. New York: Cornell UP, 2006. Print.

Gendzier, Irene L. *Frantz Fanon: A Critical Study.* New York: Pantheon Books, 1973. Print.

Gibson, Nigel C. *Fanon: The Postcolonial Imagination.* Cambridge: Polity, 2003. Print.

Gordon, Lewis R. *What Fanon Said: A Philosophical Introduction to His Life and Thought.* London: Hurst & Company, 2015. Print.

Hudis, Peter. *Frantz Fanon: Philosopher of the Barricades.* London: Pluto Press, 2015. Print.

Jean-Marie, Vivaldi. *Fanon: Collective Ethics and Humanism.* New York: Peter Lang, 2007. Print.

Lee, Christopher J. *Frantz Fanon: Toward a Revolutionary Humanism.* Athens: Ohio UP, 2015. Print.

Macey, David. *Frantz Fanon: A Life.* London: Granta Books, 2000. Print.

Nayar, Pramod K. *Frantz Fanon.* New York: Routledge, 2013. Print.

Zahar, Renate. *Frantz Fanon: Colonialism and Alienation.* Delhi: Aakar, 2010. Print.

Zeilig, Leo. *Frantz Fanon: The Militant Philosopher of Third World Revolution.* London: IB Tauris, 2014. Print.

Other books in the series

For more information, visit www.orientblackswan.com